Tony Gardiner

MATHEMATICAL
CHALLENGE

CAMBRIDGE
UNIVERSITY PRESS

CAMBRIDGE UNIVERSITY PRESS
Cambridge, New York, Melbourne, Madrid, Cape Town,
Singapore, São Paulo, Delhi, Tokyo, Mexico City

Cambridge University Press
The Edinburgh Building, Cambridge CB2 8RU, UK

Published in the United States of America by Cambridge University Press, New York

www.cambridge.org
Information on this title: www.cambridge.org/9780521558754

First published 1996
9th printing 2007

A catalogue record for this publication is available from the British Library

Library of Congress Cataloguing in Publication data
Gardiner. Tony (Anthony), 1947–
Mathematical challenge / A. Gardiner.
    p.   cm.
ISBN 978-0-521-55875-4 paperback
1. Mathematics – Problems, exercises, etc.   1. Title.
QA43.G34   1996
510′.71′2–dc20   95–43225   CIP

ISBN 978-0-521-55875-4 Paperback

Illustrations by Ralf Zeigermann
A Maxim for Vikings on page 1 from *Grooks* by Piet Hein (The MIT Press).
The quotation on page 45 from *What do you care what other people think?* by Richard
Feynman (W. W. Norton & Company, Inc.)

CONTENTS

Multiple-choice 'challenge' papers for secondary schools in the UK now involve around 300 000 pupils from 2,000 schools each year. Many schools who take part have asked for more such problems in a convenient form. This book contains past papers from the years 1988–93, together with forty-two additional sets of problems in the same style for pupils aged 11–15 – nearly six hundred problems in all.

Section A contains the annual Challenge papers, designed for the top 35% of pupils aged 11–14 (School Years 7–9 English style). As with all good mathematical problems, these can be enjoyed more widely. Most questions are accessible (under suitable conditions) to other groups of pupils aged 11–14, and many would prove challenging for older pupils. Each paper in Section A has twenty-five questions and was intended to take the very best candidates one hour to complete. Early questions on each paper are relatively straight forward, while later questions can be fairly tough. Each paper is followed by the national statistics for that year, together with some brief comments on the results. Answers are printed at the end of Section A. We produce no list of winners and no league tables of participating schools. However each school receives an analysis of its own pupils' performances, and we encourage schools to compare these statistics with the national pattern to help identify local strengths and weaknesses. Forty per cent of participants receive certificates: 6% Gold, 13% Silver, 21% Bronze. The top thousand or so candidates each year are invited to take a two-hour written follow-up paper. The problems, hints and solutions from these follow-up papers are being published separately under the title '*More mathematical challenges*' (Cambridge University Press, 1997).

Section B contains forty-two mini-papers with more problems in the same style designed for pupils aged 11–15. Each mini-paper contains ten questions, and is intended to fill a 20–30 minute class or homework slot. The papers are roughly graded: early questions on each paper, and earlier papers in Section B, tend to be easier, while later questions on each paper, and later papers in Section B, tend to be more demanding.

All the problems in the book are meant to be done *without a calculator*. Good problems make pupils *think*, and then learn from their mistakes. To reap this harvest one should actively discourage guessing, and make time to discuss the problems, solutions, and common mistakes with pupils. The introduction to Section A contains an outline of background philosophy – including an explanation of why the problems are meant to be tackled without a calculator.

Teachers will use these problems in their own way. Teaching styles vary, and different teachers have different ways of motivating their pupils, or of introducing new topics . Nevertheless most teaching and learning in mathematics involves two clearly distinct stages.

- Pupils must first understand and master some simple technique. This will often be introduced in a standard way, and then practised via a sequence of routine questions, phrased in easily recognisable language – language which is chosen to evoke a standard response.

But when pupils come to use the mathematics they know, they have to work outside the relevant chapter of the textbook – with its give-away title ('Place value', 'Angles', or whatever) and its familiar, predictable, highly suggestive language.

- Pupils therefore need to master the much more elusive skill of making mathematical sense of simple problems in the absence of give-away clues. They must learn to interpret the problems as stated, decide what has to be done, and select the relevant techniques to achieve this.

This important second stage requires regular exposure to sets of *short* problems which force pupils to think, and which cannot be solved by merely recognising key words and then applying standard tricks.

Thus, whereas the first stage involves *one-step* routine questions, in which pupils practise a standard technique, the second stage requires that pupils be regularly confronted with simple two-step (or multi-step) problems which cannot be solved by blindly applying the relevant routine method.

Ideally these two 'stages' should blend together, with the first ten routine questions on a new topic including at least one 'less routine' problem, the next ten questions including (say) three 'less routine' problems, and so on. This book contains hundreds of elementary, non-routine problems which will provide an invaluable resource for all mathematics teachers.

These sets of problems have a dual goal. They have the serious educational purpose outlined above. *But they are also meant to be fun.* Indeed, one of our main aims has been to make mathematical problems, and the experience of trying to solve them, memorable. One obvious way to achieve this is to raise the occasional smile.

Each year the 25 questions on each Challenge paper are chosen from a completely fresh set of around 150 problems. Many of these are excellent questions, but they cannot all be used. Some get left out purely by chance. Others raise important mathematical ideas, but do so in a way which demands discussion – something we cannot arrange in a large national event. Section B contains the best of these problems in a convenient form.

The annual challenge papers have a target audience of over 500 000 pupils. The multiple choice format was originally adopted to keep the operation both simple and reliable. Subsequently much care and effort has gone into finding ways of setting interesting and unusual multiple-choice problems which encourage students to think, and which penalise guessing. It should be one of the distinctive joys of school mathematics that pupils can be *sure* of their answers – even to the point of challenging the teacher's answer, or the answer in the back of the book. If pupils are to make solid progress, they must understand that mathematical problems need to be analysed carefully and logically: one should *never* resort to guessing. Once pupils begin to guess in the hope of getting the right answer (instead of thinking things through carefully), there is no longer any way for them to learn from their mistakes.

Most of the problems presented here in multiple-choice format can be adapted by deleting the five options. Many can be explored or developed in one or more ways. Some can be used as a starting point for an extended investigation. Despite this richness, all the problems are relatively short. Moreover, all have a serious mathematical core, and clear thinking is required to get at the mathematical heart of each problem. In short the educational philosophy behind these problems is totally different from that which lies behind most public examinations and official assessment tasks of recent years. I am aware of the differences and encourage readers to draw their own conclusions.

I am indebted to my colleagues in the *Problems Group* (1989–1993) – John Deft, Howard Groves, Peter Jack, Margaret Jackson, Susie Jameson and Peter Ransom – who were responsible with me for devising, stealing or adapting the original versions. Their enthusiasm, steadfastness, imagination and encouragement has been a constant source of inspiration. This book is dedicated to them.

(In response to persistent requests from schools, in 1994 the challenge for pupils aged 11–14 split in two and expanded. It now operates on two levels:

- the *UK Junior Mathematical Challenge* for School Years 8 and below;

- the *UK Intermediate Mathematical Challenge* for School Years 9, 10 and 11.

For those in Years 12 and 13 (ages 16-18) there is a similar event, the *UK Senior Mathematical Challenge* (formerly *National Mathematics Contest*).

SUPPLEMENTARY INFORMATION

One aim of these questions is for pupils to use estimation and common knowledge, and for this reason easily obtained information is often not included.

However, for those readers outside the UK, the following information might be of help:

Coins in circulation are 1p, 2p, 5p, 10p, 20p, 50p and £1. The diameter of a 1p coin is 20 mm; the diameter of a 10p coin is 24 mm. (1988 Q18; 1990 Q18 Paper 12 Q3; Paper 24 Q6; Paper 31 Q2)

Maundy Thursday is the Thursday before Easter. (1991 Q16)

A first-class stamp measures 20 mm by 25 mm; an A4 page measures 210 mm by 297 mm. (Paper 3 Q9)

The M25 motorway may be considered to be a circle of diameter 50 km (though this information is not strictly needed in order to answer the question). (Paper 8 Q9)

SECTION A

THE FIRST SIX
UK SCHOOLS MATHEMATICAL
CHALLENGE PAPERS

Here is a fact
    that should help you to fight
      a bit longer:

Things that don't act-
    ually kill you outright
      make you stronger.

            A Maxim for Vikings, Piet Hein

1988 - 1993

INTRODUCTION TO SECTION A

The *UK Schools Mathematical Challenge* started in 1988. In its first year it took place under the aegis of The Mathematical Association. From its second year it has been run by a separate organisation, the *UK Mathematics Foundation*. The following statistics give a rough idea of how the event developed during this period.

	1988	**1989**	**1990**	**1991**	**1992**	**1993**
Number of entries	16500	31500	42000	60000	80000	105000
Number of schools	340	550	750	1000	1250	1500

On the surface the UK SMC consisted of a single one-hour multiple choice paper which was taken on the first Thursday in February each year. However, as the rapid growth suggests, there is more to it than this!

Over the years the Problems Group developed a clear philosophy and a distinctive style. Though this was never formulated explicitly, it may help potential users of these problems if I highlight what I see as some important aspects of their intended spirit.

The statement of each problem is usually *short*: 'brevity is the soul of wit', and the best mathematical problems tend to reflect this fact. Mathematics is the art of identifying key variables and relationships and then subjecting them to precise analysis. This art is often best developed and tested with short, though not necessarily routine, problems (as opposed to the long-winded, pedantically structured variety which now predominate in English public exams).

The problems may be short, but they are surprisingly rich. Even where pupils choose the right answer, there may be much for them to learn by considering other, possibly more mathematical, approaches. For example: faced with the question (Section A, 1988, Question 7):

How many numbers from 1 to 100 have a figure '5' in them?

one could (a) count systematically; (b) observe that ten numbers have tens digit '5', ten numbers have units digit '5', and one number has both; or (c) work from 00 to 99 instead of 1 to 100, and count the 9×9 two-digit numbers (including those which start with 0) which do *not* use a '5'. There is mileage here for all abilities and all ages. By not providing solutions we leave to the user the pleasure of extracting the gems from this simple, but extraordinarily rich, mine.

2

The adolescent mathematical mind appreciates *elegance* and *succinctness*. In all mathematical problems some solutions are better than others. Thus, even where a pupil selects the correct option, it is always worth using class discussion to explore better approaches.

The statement of each problem may be short, but these are not routine one-step questions. Each problem needs to be *understood* and *interpreted*. Information must be selected and used in the right way. In some cases there may appear to be more than one possible interpretation. But in mathematical problems there is almost always one interpretation which is more natural than the others. Identifying this natural interpretation is part of the challenge.

In many of the problems there is an element of *surprise*. This may take different forms. The apparent setting of a problem may look familiar, but the question that is asked at the end may include an unexpected twist. Alternatively, the answer may have an unexpected simplicity. Both kinds of surprise are typical of much good mathematics. One has to be willing to look for ways of answering simple but unexpected questions by reducing them to one or more routine, familiar steps. And young mathematicians need to be immersed in, and be expected to understand, the kind of numerical 'accident' which brings a potentially inaccessible universe within the scope of mathematical analysis. Part of learning mathematics is the discovery that the numbers which emerge from good mathematical problems are often very special. This is not some regrettable feature of 'artificial problems from some pre-calculator era': it is but one aspect of 'the unreasonable effectiveness of mathematics'.

A number of problems incorporate some kind of *self-reference* (for example, Question 2 and some of the clues in Question 25 on the 1988 paper). Such questions tend to catch one off-balance: to recover one has to take a deep breath and think clearly. But problems of this kind also appeal to the human imagination, which finds self-reference fascinating – as, for example, in musical variations, Raymond Smullyan's puzzle books, or Douglas Hofstaedter's classic study *Gödel, Escher, Bach*.

Many of the problems presented here exploit the basic human appreciation of *rhyme*, and of *rhythm*. A problem in which the given data, or the names of the characters, or the context for the problem 'scan' (that is, fit together, or are commensurable with each other), is more appealing than a problem with arbitrary numbers, or with characters called X, Y and Z.

In some problems it is possible to inject an appealing element of *symmetry* (in the context; or in the options; or in the balance between the given data, the question asked and the listed options). A good problem is like good music: sometimes the individual notes fit together to make an unusually catchy tune. When they do, the impact is dramatically increased. Of course, tastes differ – in mathematics as in music.

Nevertheless, we hope that there is enough variety here to provide welcome refreshment for all maths teachers and their pupils.

At first sight some of the problems set may seem too long for a one-hour paper. But *speed* is an important part of mathematics. Faced with a mathematical problem, one may sometimes be able to find an answer by programming a machine to test all possibilities, or by making an exhaustive list. This is not good mathematics. Mathematics is the art of taming the infinite. The best solutions identify one or two key ideas and avoid the need to test cases one by one; a good approach is not only much quicker, it is more transparent and more reliable. Thus, where a problem looks too long, it is reasonable to assume that there may be shortcuts which are accessible to bright 12–14-year-olds.

Some of the problems are unashamedly 'pure', in that they are presented in terms of numbers, geometrical shapes, or whatever. Others are embedded in a *setting*. It is an important skill to be able to extract the mathematics from such a problem. But the context should serve some educational purpose: we see no point in using a context which obscures the mathematics. Moreover, the setting should make the problem *more*, not less, interesting. Our experience suggests that this is often better achieved by appealing to pupils' imagination than by pretending that the problem arose in some 'real' context. Nevertheless, we do try to ensure that each paper contains one or two problems which make pupils use their mathematics to discover something interesting about the world around them, or to reflect in a mathematical way on ordinary everyday events.

These key features of the problems, and of the cognitive and affective responses they are trying to elicit from those who work on them, are undermined when calculators are used. This is simply an observation of what happens when most students tackle such problems with access to a calculator. Calculators may well have a role to play for older students, but the dangers inherent in their use are much more serious than is generally acknowledged. Let me try to explain.

The London underground is an excellent way of getting around provided one knows exactly where one wants to go, but is interested neither in the journey itself, nor in the relation between one's destination and other familiar streets and landmarks above ground. In the same way calculators are very convenient provided one is only interested in obtaining an 'answer', and that one already understands exactly what needs to be done to obtain that answer, but is otherwise not interested in the details of the process whereby the answer is obtained. There are many occasions when these conditions are satisfied. What they all have in common is that, whenever they are satisfied, one is almost certainly interested in something other than the mathematics of the problem! Thus calculators may be natural tools in the science lab, behind the shop counter, or on a craftsman's workbench, yet be totally out of place in the mathematics classroom (most of the time). Mathematics is a *mental* universe. Learning mathematics involves exploring this universe, so to speak, 'on foot', so that one slowly learns to find one's way around. Like taxis or the tube, calculators inhibit this process by whisking one from A to B while failing to strengthen one's feeling for the intervening landscape. Yet it is precisely this 'feeling for the intervening landscape' that constitutes the mathematics behind each problem.

The options in a multiple-choice paper are sometimes referred to as *distractors*. This gives the impression of examiners trying to catch pupils out. Where a multiple-choice paper is being used to test very routine skills, this may be entirely appropriate. But where the problems are far from easy, the strategy is self-defeating. Options should be plausible; and most correspond to errors of one kind or another. But there is a difference between making a standard error in a routine calculation, and making a slip in what is in fact a fairly demanding problem. We want pupils to *think*, not to guess. Where pupils do almost exactly what one would like to see, it does not seem sensible to regularly delight in tripping them up at the very end. Thus, quite often, we *choose to omit* an option which would arise naturally as the result of such a minor slip at the very end of an otherwise correct solution. The candidate who then makes the error will realise that something has gone wrong and should be able to correct it.

The short Epilogue at the end of the book contains additional general remarks, and detailed comments on a few specific problems from the text. These remarks are included to encourage those who have already used some of the material to *reflect* on the experience and on how their pupils responded.

The Comments and Statistics section after each year's paper contains some comments which draw attention to how the national sample performed that year. I would encourage teachers to compare these comments and statistics with what they observe in their own classes.

Answers to all problems in Section A are given at the end of Section A.

These Mathematical Challenge papers are based on a few very simple *Rules* and *Guidelines*. We repeat those that are relevant here.

1.   The time allowed for each paper is 1 hour.

2.   **The use of calculators is not permitted.**

3.   *Pupils should not expect to finish the whole paper.* They should be encouraged to concentrate first on the relatively

straightforward questions 1–15. Only when they have checked their answers to these, should they attempt selected later questions.

4. The questions on these papers challenge pupils to *think*, not to guess. Pupils will get more marks (and more satisfaction) by doing one question carefully than by guessing at a lot of answers. These papers are about doing maths, not about lucky guessing.

FIRST UK SCHOOLS MATHEMATICAL CHALLENGE
1988

Questions 1–15: 5 marks each

1. Half of $99\frac{1}{2}$ is

    A $45\frac{1}{4}$ B $45\frac{3}{4}$ C $49\frac{1}{4}$ D $49\frac{1}{2}$ E $49\frac{3}{4}$

2. In this question (including all five answers) the letters 'o' and 'f' each appear

    A once B twice C three times D four times E five times

3. Harold is 8 cm taller than Jack. Jim is 12 cm shorter than Harold. Jack is 125 cm tall. How tall is Jim (in cm)?

    A 129 B 121 C 105 D 113 E 145

4. How many minutes are there between 11.41 and 14.02?

    A 141 B 261 C 241 D 221 E 361

5. The flag is given a half-turn anticlockwise about the point O and is then reflected in the dotted line. Which picture shows the correct final position of the flag?

    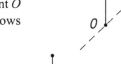

    A B C D E

6. On my calculator $\frac{1}{3} = 0.3333333$. What would $\frac{1}{30}$ be?

    A 00.333333 B 0.3030303 C 0.3333333 D 0.0303030 E 0.0333333

7. How many numbers from 1 to 100 have a figure '5' in them?

    A 10   *B* 15   *C* 19   *D* 20   *E* none of these

8. Malcolm covers any distance in one-third of the time it takes Nikki to run the same distance. They set off in opposite directions round the track as shown. Where will they meet for the first time?

    A   *B*   *C*   *D*   *E*

9. Two cats together catch sixty mice. If Rosie catches three mice for every two that Josie catches, how many does Josie catch?

    A 2   *B* 30   *C* 24   *D* 40   *E* 36

10. Which of the following is nearest to your own age, expressed in seconds?

    A 5 000 000   *B* 50 000 000   *C* 500 000 000
        D 5 000 000 000   *E* 50 000 000 000

11. Quince, quonce and quance are three types of fruit. If seven quince weigh the same as four quonce, and five quonce weigh the same as six quance, then the order of heaviness of the fruits (heaviest last) is

    A quince, quonce, quance   *B* quance, quince, quonce   *C* quonce, quance, quince
        D quonce, quince, quance   *E* quince, quance, quonce

12. A child's box of bricks contains cubes, cones and spheres. Two cones and a sphere on one side of a pair of scales will just balance a cube on the other side; and a sphere and a cube together will just balance three cones. How many spheres will just balance a single cone?

    A 1   *B* 2   *C* 3   *D* 4   *E* 5

13. A recipe for eight flapjacks needs 2 oz butter, 3 oz sugar and 4 oz rolled oats. How many flapjacks can I make if I have 14 oz butter, 15 oz sugar and 16 oz rolled oats?

    A 40   *B* 32   *C* 44   *D* 56   *E* none of these

14. Weighing the baby at the clinic was a problem. The baby would not keep still and caused the scales to wobble. So I held the baby and stood on the scales while the nurse read off 78 kg. Then the nurse held the baby while I read off 69 kg. Finally I held the nurse while the baby read off 137 kg. What is the combined weight of all three (in kg)?

    A 142   *B* 147   *C* 206   *D* 215   *E* 284

15. Arash runs faster than Betty, and Dovey will always beat Chandra in a race. Betty is never beaten by Edwina. One day all five race against each other. Just one of the following results is possible. Which is it? (ABCDE indicates 'Arash first, ...')

    A ABCDE   *B* BEDAC   *C* ABCED   *D* ADBCE   *E* ADCEB

Questions 16–25: 6 marks each

16. A quadrilateral can have four right angles. What is the largest number of right angles an octagon (8 sides) can have?

    A 6   *B* 4   *C* 2   *D* 3   *E* 8

17. How big is the angle between the hour hand and the minute hand of a clock at twenty to five?

    A 100°   *B* 25°   *C* 90°   *D* 105°   *E* 80°

18. Our class decided to raise money for charity using a 'silver line'. We invited people to put 10p pieces edge to edge to make a long line. The completed line was 25 metres long. Roughly how much money did we make?

    A £25   *B* £100   *C* £500   *D* £1000   *E* £5000

19. How many pairs of numbers of the form x, $2x+1$ are there in which both numbers are prime numbers less than 100?

    A 3   *B* 4   *C* 6   *D* 7   *E* more than 7

20. How many triangles have all three angles perfect squares (in degrees)?

    A 0   *B* 1   *C* 2   *D* 3   *E* 4

21. Which of the following has the greatest value?

    A 2^{32} *B* 4^{15} *C* 8^{11} *D* 16^{8} *E* 32^{6}

22. We can write '3 8 4' as '4 $\bar{2}$ 4', the bar indicating a negative digit (so 4 $\bar{2}$ 4 means $4\times100 - 2\times10 + 4$). How could we write 1988?

    A $2\bar{1}0\bar{2}$ *B* $200\bar{2}$ *C* $2\bar{1}2\bar{2}$ *D* $2\bar{1}\bar{1}\bar{2}$ *E* $20\bar{1}\bar{2}$

23. The dots are one unit apart. The region common to both the triangle and the square has area (in square units)

    A $\frac{9}{10}$ *B* $\frac{15}{16}$ *C* $\frac{8}{9}$ *D* $\frac{11}{12}$ *E* $\frac{14}{15}$

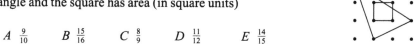

24. John, Peter, Rudolf, Susie and Tony decide to set some questions for the Schools Mathematical Challenge. John thinks up twenty-five questions and circulates them to the others. Peter, not wishing to be outdone, then sets twenty-six questions. Rudolf decides he had better get cracking and produces thirty questions. Susie sets to and comes up with thirty-nine posers, only to be beaten by Tony who produces fifty-five stunning problems. If each person takes half as long as the previous person to set each question, and Rudolf takes one hour to set all his questions, then the total time spent setting questions is

    A 7h $10\frac{1}{2}$ min   *B* 11h $34\frac{1}{2}$ min   *C* 7h 45 min
                D 2h 55 min   *E* 5h 50 min

25. A crossnumber is like a crossword except that the answers are numbers with one digit in each square.

What is the sum of the two numbers in the bottom row of the crossnumber shown?

CLUES

Across (A)
1. Prime number
3. Square of 3D

Down (D)
1. Prime number
2. Square of 1D
3. Square root of 3A

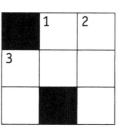

A 9   B 8   C 7   D 6   E 5

COMMENTS AND STATISTICS
1988

Statistics: The 1988 UK SMC was a 'pilot run'. While the number of entries (16 500 from 340 schools) was fairly encouraging, the internal UK SMC organisation was inevitably weak. Candidates' Answer Sheets were marked (at very short notice) by UCLES – the old Cambridge exam board – using their own marking software. The only 'statistics' which seem to have survived are the 'cut-offs' for Gold, Silver and Bronze certificates:

Gold	≥ 81 (around 6% of participants)
Silver	≥ 69 (around 13% of participants)
Bronze	≥ 57 (around 21% of participants)

In the absence of other statistics, this may be a suitable place to raise the matter of the last two *Guidelines* listed on pages 6 and 7.

3. *Pupils should not expect to finish the whole paper.* They should be encouraged to concentrate first on Questions 1–15. Only when they have checked their answers to these, should they attempt later questions.

4. The questions on these papers challenge pupils to *think*, not to guess. Pupils will get more marks (and more satisfaction) by doing one question carefully than by guessing at a lot of answers. The UK SMC is about doing maths, not about lucky guessing.

It is impossible to know exactly how these are explained to, or understood by, candidates. It does seem, however, that too many candidates fail to appreciate their significance.

There is some considerable evidence that *guessing* on non-standard problems such as these may well lead to scores *lower* than one might expect even on the basis of *random guessing*! We would like to think that both pupils and their teachers would realise that marks gained by merely guessing contradict the spirit of mathematics and the whole purpose of this particular event, whose aim is to cultivate *mathematical thinking*. (Moreover, since nothing depends on the result of this particular test, there is no *external* reason for adopting such tactics.)

SECOND UK SCHOOLS MATHEMATICAL CHALLENGE
1989

Questions 1–15: 5 marks each

1. If the following fractions are written in order of size, which will be in the middle?

    A $\frac{1}{3}$ B $\frac{3}{10}$ C 31% D 0.03 E 0.303

2. I start counting at 19 and go on to 89, taking one second to say each number. How long do I take altogether?

    A 1 min 10 s B 1 min 29 s C 1 min 11 s D 1 min 19 s E 1 min exactly

3. The diagram shows a regular pentagon with two of its diagonals. If *all* the diagonals are drawn in, into how many areas will the pentagon be divided?

    A 4 B 8 C 11 D 10 E 5

4. The names of the whole numbers from one to twelve are written down in the order they occur in a dictionary. What is the fourth number on the list?

    A four B five C six D seven E nine

5. The graph shows how the weight of a letter (including the envelope) varies with the number of sheets of paper used.
    What is the weight of a single sheet of paper?

    A 5 g B 10 g C 15 g D 20 g E 25 g

6. In a magic square, the three numbers in each row, in each
   column, and in each diagonal add up to the same number.
   When the magic square shown here is completed, which of
   the following numbers is not used?

13		
	10	
9		7

   A 6   *B* 8   *C* 12   *D* 14   *E* 15

7. Which of these numbers is the average (mean) of the other four?

   A 28   *B* 30   *C* 26   *D* 37   *E* 29

8. The square has area 36 cm². What is the area (in cm²) of its
   inscribed circle?

   A 6π   *B* 9π   *C* 12π   *D* 36π   *E* 81π

9. An ant is crawling in a straight line from one corner of a table to the opposite corner
   when he bumps into a one centimetre cube of sugar. Instead of crawling round it,
   or eating his way through it, he climbs straight up and over it before continuing on
   his intended route. How much does the detour add to the expected length of his
   journey?

   A 1 cm   *B* 2 cm   *C* 3 cm   *D* 4 cm   *E* 5 cm

10. The date 8 November 1988 was unusual. If we write it in the form 8/11/88, we have
    8 × 11 = 88. How many such dates were there in 1990?

    A 5   *B* 4   *C* 3   *D* 2   *E* 1

11. I want to read the coded message shown here. I know that
    each number stands for a letter, but I have lost the 'key'. All
    I can remember is that 26 stands for 'A' and that 5 stands for
    'V'. What does 23 stand for?

    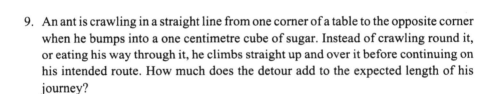
    26 5 12 18 23
    26 25 24 22

    A   *B*   *C*   *D*   *E*

12. One million is approximately the number of

A grains of sand on a beach   B seconds in a day   C people in England and Wales
        D grains of sugar in a cupful   E blades of grass on a football pitch

13. The Kryptor Faction required competitors to choose one of
    these five jigsaw pieces and to fit it into the hole on the right
    without turning the piece over. Which is the correct piece?

A   B   C   D   E

14. Baby's nearly one year old now. We've worked out how to weigh her but nurse and
    I still have trouble measuring her height. She just *will* not stand up straight against
    our measuring chart. In fact she can't stand up at all yet! So we measure her upside
    down. Last year nurse held Baby's feet, keeping them level with the 140 cm mark,
    while I read off the mark level with the top of Baby's head: 97 cm. This year it was
    my turn to hold the feet. Being taller than nurse, I held them against the 150 cm
    mark, while nurse crawled on the floor to read the mark level with the top of Baby's
    head: 84 cm. How many centimetres has Baby grown in her first year?

    A 13   B 237   C 53   D 23   E 66

15. In the diagram the lengths SP, SQ and SR are equal and the
    angle SRQ is $x°$. What is the size (in degrees) of angle PQR?

    A 90   B $2x$ C $3x$ D $180 - x$ E $180 - 2x$

Questions 16–25: 6 marks each

16. This grid can be filled up using only the numbers 1, 2, 3, 4,
    5 so that each number appears just once in each row, once in
    each column, and once in each diagonal. Which number
    goes in the centre square?

    A 1   B 2   C 3   D 4   E 5

17. A car with five tyres (four road tyres and a spare) travelled 30 000 km. All five tyres were used equally. How many kilometres' wear did each tyre receive?

    A 6000   *B* 7500   *C* 24 000   *D* 30 000   *E* 150 000

18. When a 16 by 9 rectangle is cut as shown here the pieces can be rearranged to make a square of perimeter

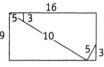

    A 32   *B* 36   *C* 40   *D* 48   *E* 51

19. Our school dinners offer the same basic choice each day. *Starters*: soup or fruit juice; *Main course*: meat, fish, salad, chicken or curry; *Afters*: crumble, cake or sponge. I change my choice of course each day, trying each option in turn, going back to soup after fruit juice, to meat after curry and to crumble after sponge. Today, to celebrate the 2nd UK SMC, I shall sit down to soup, meat and crumble. How many school dinners will I have eaten before I next sit down to the same combination?

    A 3   *B* 5   *C* 10   *D* 15   *E* 30

20. A knitted scarf uses three balls of wool. I start the day with b balls of wool and knit s scarves. How many balls of wool do I have at the end of the day?

    A $3(b-s)$ *B* $b-3-s$ *C* $b-3s$ *D* $3bs$ *E* $s+3b$

21. A stone is dropped from the top of a tower. Which graph shows how its speed changes with time up to the moment when it hits the ground?

22. When Ann stands on Ben's shoulders she can just see over a wall. When Ben stands on Con's shoulders he can see nothing but bricks. When Con stands on Den's shoulders she can see over easily. Who are the tallest and the shortest?

    A Ann & Ben   *B* Den & Con   *C* Den & Ben
            D Ann & Con   *E* can't be sure

23. What fraction of the area of the regular hexagon is the shaded triangle?

A $\frac{1}{4}$ $\qquad$ B $\frac{1}{3}$ $\qquad$ C $\frac{3}{8}$ $\qquad$ D $\frac{5}{12}$ $\qquad$ E $\frac{1}{2}$

24. A crossnumber is like a crossword except that the answers are numbers with one digit in each square.

What is the sum of all the digits in the solution to this crossnumber?

CLUES
Across (A)
1. See 3D
3. Cube
4. 5 times 3D
Down (D)
2. Square
3. 4 times 1A

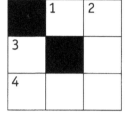

A 15 $\qquad$ B 17 $\qquad$ C 23 $\qquad$ D 26 $\qquad$ E can't be sure

25. How many patches (pentagons and hexagons) were stitched together to make this football?

A 15 $\qquad$ B 19 $\qquad$ C 30 $\qquad$ D 32 $\qquad$ E 34

COMMENTS AND STATISTICS
1989

Statistics: The 1989 UK SMC attracted 31 500 entries from 550 schools. The cut-offs for the award of certificates were as follows:

Gold	≥ **88**	(around 6% of participants)
Silver	≥ **76**	(around 13% of participants)
Bronze	≥ **64**	(around 21% of participants)

Since 1989 each participating school has received detailed statistics as well as results and certificates. These indicate the options chosen by its own pupils and the percentage of participants nationally who chose each option in each question. We believe these statistics – especially the national figures and any differences between the pattern of choices in a particular school and the pattern nationally – can be enlightening. We would like the UK SMC to stimulate discussion of these statistics by teachers in participating schools. The percentage responses given below show the percentage of participants nationally who chose each option. Against '0' we give the percentage who omitted that particular question; against '2+' we give the percentage of participants who marked more than one option. The 'correct' option for each question is underlined.

Qn:	1	2	3	4	5	6	7	8	9	10	11	12	13	14	15
A	7.7	71.2	2.1	53.4	38.6	2.5	5.8	19.3	1.4	21.9	0.5	2.3	8.0	15.8	34.3
B	22.8	1.8	9.8	8.9	5.4	2.1	69.9	25.9	17.1	16.9	1.3	29.6	18.7	0.5	18.5
C	21.2	20.6	64.7	5.0	52.6	2.0	6.0	26.0	70.7	14.3	10.1	9.7	44.2	1.8	10.4
D	7.3	2.0	5.1	19.7	0.4	2.5	3.4	15.6	0.6	25.2	78.9	34.2	10.1	71.1	15.8
E	35.8	2.2	15.3	9.7	0.4	86.4	9.2	2.8	7.7	16.3	3.7	17.5	15.1	6.1	11.3
0	4.5	1.6	2.1	2.7	2.1	3.6	5.2	9.5	2.1	4.6	5.1	5.9	3.1	4.3	9.2
2+	0.6	0.5	0.7	0.6	0.5	0.9	0.4	0.8	0.5	0.8	0.4	0.8	0.8	0.5	0.6

Qn:	16	17	18	19	20	21	22	23	24	25
A	20.1	71.7	5.3	5.7	18.0	22.4	5.0	10.5	3.8	2.9
B	41.6	4.2	18.8	13.3	9.1	11.5	35.7	45.3	7.9	9.5
C	10.9	15.8	13.1	16.8	33.9	15.8	26.6	14.0	10.7	19.9
D	8.8	3.4	27.7	13.5	14.6	12.8	4.5	13.4	11.2	40.1
E	7.8	1.2	17.3	41.6	10.9	26.7	17.5	1.9	43.0	13.6
0	9.4	2.9	17.0	8.0	12.7	9.7	9.4	14.0	22.4	13.2
2+	1.4	0.7	1.0	1.1	0.8	1.1	1.2	0.8	1.1	0.9

The responses to the relatively straightforward **Q2, Q5** and **Q17**, and to the very basic **Q1**, stand out. Some of the more popular, but misguided, preferences (2A ('posts and gaps'!), 3E, 4D(!), 5C, 8C (doubly erroneous!), 8AD, 9C, 12BE, 15BCD, 18BCE) should also provide much food for thought. Teachers who use these problems with their own classes might like to compare these errors with those made by their own pupils, and reflect on how they can be avoided.

THIRD UK SCHOOLS MATHEMATICAL CHALLENGE
1990

Questions 1–15: 5 marks each

1. Suppose we arrange the five numbers 1, 2, 3, 4, 5 in the five squares so that the horizontal and vertical lines both add to 8. Which number has to go in the middle square?

    A 1 B 2 C 3 D 4 E 5

2. We are told that 20% of the sixty million people in the UK watch *Neighbours*. Roughly how many million people is that?

    A 1.2 B 3 C 12 D 15 E 33

3. Which of the following is a *wrong* description of the '5' in 500 396?

    A 500 000 ones B 5000 hundreds C 500 thousands
         D 50 ten thousands E 5 millions

4. Lewis starts in square L facing 'north'. He moves one square forward, turns to his right, moves one square forward, turns to his left and moves one square forward again. Where does he land up?

    A B C D E

5. I am thinking of a rule that converts the number 6 into the number 20. Which of the following could *not* be my rule?

    A add 14 B take half then add 17 C treble then add 2
         D add 4 then square E subtract 2 then multiply by 5

6. Two dice are thrown and the scores are added together. What is the most likely total?

   A 6   B 7   C 9   D 12   E all results are equally likely

7. Bilbo and Frodo have just consumed a plateful of cherries. Each repeats the rhyme 'Tinker, tailor, soldier, sailor, rich man, poor man, beggar man, thief' over and over again as he runs through his own heap of cherry stones. Bilbo finishes on 'sailor', whereas Frodo finishes on 'poor man'. What would they have finished on if they had run through both heaps together?

   A tinker   B tailor   C soldier   D thief   E can't be sure

8. I bought seven packets of biscuits. Each packet cost the same and at the till I got 4p change. How much did I give the cashier?

   A £1   B £2   C £3   D £4   E £5

9. *Mathematical Pie* is a magazine for pupils at school. The cost per copy depends on how many copies a school orders. In 1990, 1 copy cost 32p; 2 copies cost 23p each; 3–6 copies cost 20p each; 7–39 copies cost 17p each; 40–149 copies cost 16p each. If your school bought 18 copies of one issue, how much change would they have got from £10?

   A £3.06   B £4.24   C £5.86   D £6.94   E £9.83

10. In a triangle the smallest angle is 20°. What is the largest possible angle in the triangle?

    A 80°   B 90°   C 140°   D 159°   E 160°

11. The net shown here is cut out and folded to form a cube. Which face is then opposite the face marked X?

    A   B   C   D   E

12. Tony owes Tina 40p. Then Tina borrows 50p from Tony. Later Tony gives Tina 60p. Who has to pay what to whom to square things up?

    A Tony gives Tina £1.50   *B* Tony gives Tina 70p   *C* Tony gives Tina 50p
           D Tina gives Tony 70p   *E* Tony gives Tina 30p

13. The diagram shows a reindeer made from five matches. You have to move just one match to make another similar reindeer. Which match should you move?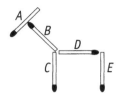

    A   *B*   *C*   *D*   *E*

14. Baby's two years old now and drinks milk by the quarter pint, so we have decided to call her *GILL*. Getting her to recognise her name proved difficult, so we put the four letters *G, I, L, L* on separate building blocks. She loves arranging them, but rarely gets them in the right order. One day she managed to produce every possible four-letter 'word': $\boxed{L}\boxed{I}\boxed{L}\boxed{G}$ is one such. How many different four-letter words did she produce that day?

    A 3   *B* 4   *C* 12   *D* 16   *E* 24

15. The graph shows the distance travelled by a car against the time taken. What does the graph show the car is doing?

    A speeding up   *B* standing still   *C* travelling north-east
          D travelling uphill   *E* travelling at a steady speed

Questions 16–25: 6 marks each

16. One holiday weekend last spring, the AA reported a traffic jam 12 miles long on one carriageway of the M25. Assuming that all three lanes were affected, roughly how many cars were involved in the jam?

    A 2000   *B* 6000   *C* 20 000   *D* 60 000   *E* 100 000

17. The measures of length in ancient Rome included the *pes*, the *passus* and the *stadium*. 5 *pedes* = 1 *passus*, 125 *passus* = 1 *stadium*. The atrium (courtyard) of Marcus' home was a square with each side 50 *pedes* long. How many times did Marcus have to walk round his atrium to complete his daily exercise of 8 *stadia*?

    A XX   *B* XXV   *C* L   *D* C   *E* CXXV

18. In how many ways can you give change for a ten pence piece?

    A 6   *B* 7   *C* 9   *D* 10   *E* 12

19. A car can go r miles on s gallons of petrol. How many gallons of petrol would it need for a journey of t miles?

    $A\ \dfrac{st}{r}$ $B\ \dfrac{rs}{t}$ $C\ \dfrac{tr}{s}$ $D\ \dfrac{r}{st}$ $E\ \dfrac{t}{sr}$

20. The table shows the distance (in km) between five towns in southern France. Five friends live in these five towns and want to meet. In which town should they meet to keep the total travelling distance as small as possible?

Bergerac				
87	Bordeaux			
79	47	Langon		
61	31	54	Libourne	
58	84	37	65	Marmande

    A Bergerac   *B* Bordeaux   *C* Langon   *D* Libourne   *E* Marmande

21. Some small equilateral triangles are fitted together to make one large equilateral triangle. The large triangle is shown here partly covered by a sheet of paper. How many small triangles were used altogether?

    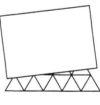

    A 12   *B* 13   *C* 15   *D* 25   *E* 45

22. Both 4 and 8 can be written as the sum of two prime numbers (4 = 2 + 2, 8 = 3 + 5). How many numbers less than 20 cannot be written as the sum of two prime numbers?

    A 3   *B* 5   *C* 6   *D* 7   *E* 8

23. Ali (A) and Baba (B) are shown surrounded by six thieves. The thieves' ages are given. Ali's age is the average of his four nearest neighbours, and so is Baba's. How old is Ali?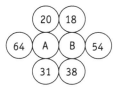

   A 37   B $37\frac{1}{2}$ C $38\frac{1}{3}$ D $42\frac{1}{4}$ E 38

24. The symbol 50! represents the product of all the whole numbers from 1 to 50 inclusive; that is, $50! = 1 \times 2 \times 3 \times \ldots \times 49 \times 50$. If I were to calculate the actual value, how many zeros would the answer have at the end?

   A 12   B 11   C 10   D 6   E 5

25. Which of the cubes shown could be made from this net?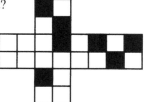

A   B   C   D   E

Statistics: The 1990 UK SMC attracted 42 000 entries from 750 schools. The paper was intended to be slightly easier than the previous year's. The cut-off scores for the award of certificates this year were as follows:

Gold	≥ 97	(around 6% of participants)
Silver	≥ 86	(around 13% of participants)
Bronze	≥ 76	(around 21% of participants)

The percentage of participants choosing the five options for each question were as follows. (Please refer to the 1989 Comments and Statistics if the layout is not clear.)

Qn:	1	2	3	4	5	6	7	8	9	10	11	12	13	14	15
A	<u>94.1</u>	6.7	5.3	17.1	1.5	6.3	6.9	4.7	11.2	8.0	2.1	0.6	41.4	7.6	23.0
B	2.1	18.8	8.9	4.2	1.9	<u>27.6</u>	<u>35.9</u>	<u>68.5</u>	2.9	12.3	1.4	2.7	15.7	7.1	1.0
C	2.3	<u>61.7</u>	8.5	<u>76.3</u>	2.2	3.4	3.9	11.9	3.1	<u>27.2</u>	2.3	5.7	8.5	<u>54.7</u>	4.7
D	0.5	7.6	8.6	1.5	<u>92.0</u>	2.0	7.4	7.2	<u>74.0</u>	38.0	5.5	<u>88.1</u>	4.3	19.7	3.6
E	0.7	4.3	<u>67.7</u>	0.5	1.9	59.8	44.2	4.9	7.2	13.2	<u>88.0</u>	2.4	<u>23.9</u>	9.6	<u>67.0</u>
0	0.3	0.8	0.7	0.3	0.4	0.7	1.6	2.6	1.5	1.1	0.6	0.4	6.0	1.2	0.5
2+	0.0	0.1	0.3	0.1	0.1	0.2	0.1	0.1	0.1	0.1	0.1	0.1	0.2	0.2	0.1

Qn:	16	17	18	19	20	21	22	23	24	25
A	8.6	12.3	10.1	<u>17.0</u>	3.3	0.6	25.2	11.0	<u>12.0</u>	<u>29.0</u>
B	<u>24.1</u>	<u>36.8</u>	7.8	26.9	10.2	0.7	<u>20.0</u>	17.6	11.4	13.3
C	28.1	12.4	24.5	19.5	25.7	6.2	14.2	28.0	18.8	4.5
D	21.7	22.4	<u>34.8</u>	8.0	<u>44.1</u>	<u>79.9</u>	9.9	10.0	15.2	25.6
E	7.0	8.3	19.2	17.2	5.0	6.5	14.4	<u>13.6</u>	19.6	12.2
0	10.3	7.6	3.4	11.2	11.5	5.9	16.0	19.6	22.7	14.9
2+	0.2	0.2	0.3	0.3	0.2	0.2	0.3	0.2	0.3	0.5

What is interesting in these statistics is not just the percentage getting a particular question *right* or *wrong*, but the distribution of responses, and the response patterns in different, but related, problems. Among the more basic questions the responses to **Q2**, **Q3**, **Q6**, **Q7** and **Q10** should provide food for thought. Common errors (2B, 4A, 6E(!), 7E(!), 8C, 10D, 13AB, 14D and 15A) challenge all of us to reflect on what can so easily go wrong. Since the UK SMC is aimed at the top 35% of pupils aged 11–14, the responses to **Q18**, **Q19** and **Q23** also raise a number of issues.

FOURTH UK SCHOOLS MATHEMATICAL CHALLENGE
1991

Questions 1–15: 5 marks each

1. Four of the options are equal. Which is the odd one out?

   $A \ \ 1 \div 9 + 9 \div 1$ $B \ \ 1 \times 9 \div (9 \times 1)$ $C \ \ 1 - 9 + 9 \times 1$

        $D \ \ 1 + 9 \div 9 - 1$ $E \ \ 1 \times (9 - 9) + 1$

2. How many squares are there altogether in this diagram?

   A 8 B 9 C 10 D 11 E 12

3. I set my video recorder to record the late film from 11.15 pm to 1.05 am. How many minutes of the new 4 hour tape remained unused?

   A 50 B 110 C 130 D 150 E 190

4. Four of the following are equal. Which is the odd one out?

   $A \ \ \frac{1}{3} + \frac{5}{7}$ B 0.6 $C \ \ \frac{15}{25}$ D 60% $E \ \ \frac{1}{2} + \frac{1}{10}$

5. Here are the dates of three mathematicians: Sophie Germain (French) 1776–1831, Sonja Kowalevsky (Russian) 1850–91, Emmy Noether (German) 1882–1935. Arrange them in order with the shortest-lived first (for example, GKN would mean Germain was the youngest when she died and Noether the eldest).

   A GNK B NGK C KGN D NKG E KNG

6. Looking in at the greengrocer's window it said '**POTATOES**'. When I went inside and looked from the other side, what did I see?

    A **ƎOTATOƧ**   *B* **ꙄƎOTATOꟼ**   *C* **POTATOES**

    D **ꙄƎOTATOꟼ**   *E* **ꙄƎOTATOꟼ**

7. Rachel arranges the fingers of her right hand so that her thumb points upwards, her first finger points north and her second finger points west: we write this for short as 'TU, 1N, 2W'. She then keeps her fingers fixed like this, but can twist her arm and wrist if she likes. Which of the following can she *not* achieve? (D = down, S = south, E = east)

    A TD, 1N, 2E   *B* TN, 1D, 2W   *C* TS, 1E, 2U
              D TE, 1U, 2S   *E* TW, 1S, 2D

8. Four of the points with these coordinates lie on a single straight line. Which is the odd one out?

    A (6, 11)   *B* (5, 5)   *C* (4, 7)   *D* (8, 15)   *E* (2, 3)

9. How big is the angle x?

    A 30°   *B* 36°   *C* 44°   *D* 45°   *E* 64°

10. Nine bus stops are equally spaced along a bus route. The distance from the first to the third is 600 m. How far is it from the first to the last?

    A 600 m   *B* 1600 m   *C* 1800 m   *D* 2400 m   *E* 2700 m

11. In 1990 a new size 5p coin was minted. The old size weighed 5.65 g while the new size weighs 3.25 g. How much lighter will your pocket be if it contains £5 worth of the new size coins instead of the old size?

    A 2.4000 g   *B* 24 g   *C* 12 g   *D* 240 g   *E* no difference

12. A *rod* (sometimes called a *pole*, or a *perch*) was an old unit of length. To measure a rod you were to stand outside a church on a Sunday morning, stop the first sixteen men to come out, and line them up with their left feet in one long line touching toe to heel: the distance from the front to the back of this line was called a *rod*. The *exact* length you got depended on who went to church that day, but it was always more or less the same length. How long was a rod to the nearest metre?

A 4 m B 5 m C 6 m D 7 m E 8 m

13. How many of these statements are true?

(i) $12 \div \frac{1}{2} = 6$ (ii) $3\% = 0.3$ (iii) $\frac{1}{7} < \frac{1}{9}$ (iv) $0.2 \times 0.4 = 0.8$

A none B one C two D three E four

14. Sound travels at about 330 metres per second; light travels so fast that it arrives almost instantaneously. If you time the gap between a flash of lightning and its clap of thunder as 6 seconds, roughly how far away is the storm?

A 55 m B 330 m C 1 km D 2 km E 6 km

15. What is the angle between the two hands of a clock at 2.30?

A 100° B 105° C 110° D 120° E 135°

Questions 16–25: 6 marks each

16. Every Maundy Thursday the reigning monarch distributes 'Maundy money' to equal numbers of men and women. Last year at Newcastle 64 men and 64 women each received 64p, one penny for each year of the Queen's life. Written as a power of 2, what was the total amount distributed in pence?

A 2^6 B 2^7 C 2^{12} D 2^{13} E 2^{42}

17. Snow White wanted to know the mean height of the Seven Dwarves. So one day she measured them all as they left for work and calculated their mean height (correct to one decimal place) as 112.3 cm. Doc complained that she had missed him out and had measured Dopey twice without him noticing. If Doc is 3 cm taller than Dopey, what is the mean height of the Seven Dwarves?

A 111.9 cm   *B* 112.3 cm   *C* 112.7 cm   *D* 113.8 cm   *E* 115.3 cm

18. Each letter stands for a different digit. Which letter has the lowest value?

A U   *B* K   *C* S   *D* M   *E* C

19. The seven pieces in this 12 cm × 12 cm square make a Tangram set. What is the area of the shaded parallelogram?

A 6 cm²   *B* 12 cm²   *C* 18 cm²   *D* 36 cm²   *E* 144 cm²

20. A quiz has twenty questions with seven points awarded for each correct answer, two points deducted for each wrong answer and zero for each question omitted. Jack scores 87 points. How many questions did he omit?

A 2   *B* 5   *C* 7   *D* 9   *E* 13

21. The perimeter of a large triangle is 24 cm. What is the total length of the black lines used to draw the figure?

A 57 cm   *B* 66 cm   *C* 75 cm   *D* 78 cm   *E* 81 cm

22. 4 star petrol at s pence per litre costs 3 pence per litre more than unleaded. How many pence does it cost to buy u litres of unleaded petrol?

A $u(s-3)$ *B* $s+3$ *C* $s-3$ *D* $us-3$ *E* $(4s+3)u$

23. Which of the following could this graph *not* represent?

A x = time after midnight, y = depth of water in the harbour
B x = time after throwing, y = speed of a rock falling down a well
C x = weight in grams, y = weight in ounces
D x = temperature in °C, y = temperature in °F
E x = age of child, y = height of that child

24. Fill the empty squares with As, Bs, Cs, Ds, Es so that no line (horizontal, vertical or inclined at 45°) contains a letter more than once. Which letter goes in the square marked ⋆?

    A   B   C   D   E

	⋆	A		
	E			B
		C		

25. If all plinks are plonks and some plunks are plinks, which of the statements X, Y, Z *must* be true?

X: All plinks are plonks
Y: Some plonks are plunks
Z: Some plinks are not plunks

A X only   B Y only   C Z only   D X & Y only   E Y & Z only

COMMENTS AND STATISTICS
1991

Statistics: There were 60 000 entries from almost 1000 schools. The cut-off scores for certificates and the detailed results were as follows:

Gold	$\geq$ **91**	(around 6% of participants)
Silver	$\geq$ **74**	(around 13% of participants)
Bronze	$\geq$ **59**	(around 21% of participants)

The percentage of participants choosing the five options for each question were as follows:

Qn:	1	2	3	4	5	6	7	8	9	10	11	12	13	14	15
A	38.4	17.2	1.7	55.7	10.9	6.8	17.0	2.7	4.3	0.4	9.7	34.0	11.6	7.9	8.3
B	8.4	1.3	12.5	4.9	3.1	13.7	15.8	77.2	9.2	4.6	13.7	30.3	20.9	4.7	19.7
C	15.7	1.0	61.5	18.4	9.6	1.8	27.7	8.1	10.6	46.1	8.3	13.3	32.5	6.5	10.2
D	22.9	77.3	11.0	4.6	3.1	76.3	12.7	5.3	3.8	37.5	65.0	5.3	27.0	57.6	45.9
E	10.8	2.8	12.5	13.4	71.6	1.0	20.8	3.5	69.8	10.9	1.3	13.6	6.8	21.0	14.9
0	3.8	0.4	1.0	3.1	1.7	0.5	5.3	3.2	2.3	0.6	2.1	3.5	1.1	2.4	1.1
2+	0.1	0.1	0.1	0.1	0.2	0.1	1.1	0.1	0.2	0.0	0.1	0.1	0.1	0.1	0.1

Qn:	16	17	18	19	20	21	22	23	24	25
A	13.7	5.2	4.7	16.7	9.2	8.4	46.0	17.5	2.3	7.6
B	8.9	7.8	22.3	14.2	26.8	12.6	8.6	26.1	30.2	11.3
C	19.5	33.5	23.7	42.7	24.0	11.6	13.8	20.6	17.6	24.2
D	22.8	9.7	20.0	10.1	10.8	17.4	10.7	10.3	26.5	9.8
E	21.1	36.2	19.6	2.6	13.3	29.6	6.0	10.6	3.0	34.3
0	14.0	7.6	9.8	13.8	15.8	20.4	14.9	14.4	20.4	12.6
2+	0.2	0.2	0.2	0.2	0.2	0.3	0.2	0.6	0.2	0.2

Questions like **Q2** were clearly fairly familiar. However **Q1, Q3, Q4, Q10, Q13** and **Q15** would – quite rightly – be seen by many as being more fundamental, and the responses correspondingly more significant. One suspects that no work at all is done on the ubiquitous mathematical idea of counting 'posts and gaps' (**Q10**); for example, 'How many whole numbers are there strictly between 67 and 152?' The fact that our 'National' Curriculum ignores, undervalues and misrepresents many important mathematical ideas and techniques certainly makes the teacher's task more difficult. But if we want to lay the mathematical foundations for subsequent work and employment, we must somehow make time to cover key topics more effectively (**Q1, Q4, Q10, Q13** and **Q15**).

In some repects the paper was harder than last year's (there were fewer easy questions); in other respects the paper was definitely *easier* (with *nine* perfect scores compared with *one* in 1990 and *none* in 1988 or 1989).

FIFTH UK SCHOOLS MATHEMATICAL CHALLENGE
1992

Questions 1–15: 5 marks each

1. This part of the UK SMC logo can be drawn without taking your pencil off the paper and without going over any line twice. If you start at *S*, at which corner will you finish?

   A U   *B* K   *C* S   *D* M   *E* C

2. Deirdre should have divided a number by 4, but instead she subtracted 4. She got the answer 48. What should her answer have been?

   A 12   *B* 13   *C* 52   *D* 192   *E* 208

3. Forty years ago today (6 February 1992) King George VI died and his eldest daughter Elizabeth acceded to the throne aged twenty-five. Her birthday is on 21 April. In which year was she born?

   A 1926   *B* 1927   *C* 1952   *D* 1966   *E* 1967

4. Twelve million twelve thousand twelve hundred and twelve can be written as

   A 12 012 012   *B* 12 013 212   *C* 12 121 212
         D 120 121 212   *E* 133 212

5. *M* is the midpoint of the side of the rectangle. What is the area (in square units) of the triangle *PMR*?

   A 3   *B* 5   *C* 6   *D* 10   *E* 12

6. 'Think of any whole number. Double it and add five. Double this answer and then add two. Now take away the number you first thought of.' Then, no matter which number you start with, your answer will always be

    A even   *B* a multiple of 3   *C* a multiple of 5
           D a multiple of 6   *E* odd

7. I have a max/min thermometer in my greenhouse. It records both the highest and the lowest temperatures reached from the time I reset it. I reset it on Sunday when the temperature was 4°C. Overnight the temperature fell 5°. Then during Monday it rose by 6° before falling 10° during the night. On Tuesday it rose by 4° and fell 2° overnight. On Wednesday it rose 8° during the day. When I looked at it on Wednesday evening, what were the maximum and minimum temperatures recorded?

    A 12° and −6°   *B* 1° and −9°   *C* 10° and 0°
          D 5° and 4°   *E* 5° and −5°

8. In a village the pub is 300 m due north of the school, and the church is 300 m from the pub on a bearing 060. What is the bearing of the school from the church?

    A 030   *B* 120   *C* 210   *D* 240   *E* 300

9. I am standing behind five pupils who are signalling a five-digit number to someone on the opposite side of the playground. From where I am standing the number looks like 23456. What number is actually being signalled?

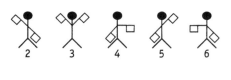

    A 42635   *B* 45632   *C* 53624   *D* 62435   *E* 65432

10. The fraction $\frac{16}{64}$ is unusual since the digit 6, which occurs on both the top and the bottom, can be 'cancelled' to give $\frac{1}{4}$ and this is equal to $\frac{16}{64}$. Which of these fractions has a similar property?

    A $\frac{12}{24}$ *B* $\frac{13}{39}$ *C* $\frac{15}{45}$ *D* $\frac{19}{95}$ *E* $\frac{24}{48}$

11. *ABCD* is a square. *P* and *Q* are points outside the square such that triangles *ABP* and *BCQ* are both equilateral. How big is angle *PQB*?

    A 10°   *B* 15°   *C* 20°   *D* 25°   *E* 30°

12. The total weight of five ballet dancers is 425 kg and the average (mean) weight of ten rugby players is 40 kg. What is the average weight of all fifteen people?

    A 31 kg   *B* 55 kg   *C* 62.5 kg   *D* 75 kg   *E* 89 kg

13. A piece of paper 16 cm by 32 cm is cut in half. One of these pieces is cut in half again, and the process is repeated until a piece 1 cm by 2 cm is eventually obtained. How many cuts are needed altogether?

    A 4   *B* 6   *C* 8   *D* 10   *E* can't be sure

14. Gill's back! This year was her fourth birthday. The highlight of her party was a game of musical chairs. The game got down to herself, nurse and me. Only two chairs were left – the hard chair and the comfy chair, with a big gap between them. The music stopped and we all piled onto the nearest chair, some on top of one another. If Gill's bottom was firmly in contact with one of the two chairs, in how many different ways could this have happened?

    A 4   *B* 6   *C* 8   *D* 10   *E* 12

15. The diagram shows a 30 cm ruler balanced on two pencils: the left pencil is at the 10 cm mark and the right pencil is at the 25 cm mark. If I move the pencils slowly towards each other, keeping the ruler balanced on them, what will happen?

    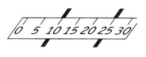

    A   both pencils slide simultaneously and meet at the 15 cm mark
    B   both pencils slide simultaneously and meet at the 17.5 cm mark
    C   my left pencil slides to the 15 cm mark, then my right slides to join it
    D   my right pencil slides to the 15 cm mark, then my left slides to join it
    E   the pencils slide alternately till they meet at the 15 cm mark

16. At which of these times are the two hands of a clock closest to being on top of each other?

    A 6.30   *B* 6.31   *C* 6.32   *D* 6.33   *E* 6.34

17. Ahmed, Brian, Chloe, Danielle, Ethel, Francis and George have to choose a Form Captain from among themselves. They decide to stand in a circle, in alphabetical order, and to count round (in the same order) rejecting every third person they come to; that person then leaves the circle. The last one left is to be Form Captain. Ahmed is eventually elected Form Captain. Where must the counting have started?

    A Ahmed   *B* Brian   *C* Danielle   *D* Ethel   *E* George

18. Humphrey the horse at full stretch is hard to match. But that is just what you have to do: move one match to make another horse just like (i.e. congruent to) Humphrey. Which match must you move?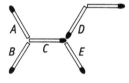

    A   *B*   *C*   *D*   *E*

19. A simple code uses numbers in place of letters, with 1 standing for A, 2 for B, 3 for C and so on up to 26 for Z. Code words are written without spaces, so '12' could mean either AB or L. Which of these messages can decode to only one English word?

    A 12125   *B* 25519   *C* 135   *D* 208919   *E* 8514

20. 'As I was going to St Ives I met a man with seven wives; each wife had seven sacks; each sack had seven cats; each cat had seven kits ...' If it costs 10p per day to feed each kit and 20p per day to feed each cat, what is the man's daily pet-food bill?

    A £2.10   *B* £6.30   *C* £44.10   *D* £88.20   *E* £308.70

21. A two-digit number is divided by the sum of its digits. What is the largest possible remainder?

 A 9   *B* 13   *C* 15   *D* 16   *E* 17

22. The Greek mathematician Eratosthenes noticed that on a certain day at noon the sun was directly overhead in Syene (he could see its reflection in the water at the bottom of a deep well!), while in Alexandria at the same time on the same day the sun's rays made an angle of 7° with the vertical. He knew that Alexandria was 5000 stades north of Syene and used this to calculate the circumference of the Earth. What was Eratosthenes' estimate (in stades) for the circumference of the Earth?

 A 5000   *B* 26 000   *C* 35 000   *D* 40 000   *E* 260 000

23. In the figure, $\frac{3}{4}$ of the smaller square is shaded and $\frac{6}{7}$ of the larger square is shaded. What is the ratio of the shaded area of the smaller square to the shaded area of the larger square?

 A $\frac{1}{2}$ *B* $\frac{4}{7}$ *C* $\frac{3}{4}$ *D* $\frac{6}{7}$ *E* $\frac{7}{8}$

24. Four comrades are racing side by side down a dusty staircase. Frodo goes down two steps at a time, Gimli three, Legolas four and Aragorn five. If the only steps with all four's footprints are at the top and the bottom, how many steps have just one footprint?

 A 16   *B* 17   *C* 20   *D* 22   *E* 44

25. One of the most popular arithmetic books of all time (*The Scholar's Guide to Arithmetic* by Bonnycastle, 6th edition 1795) contains the exercise: 'If a cardinal can pray a soul out of purgatory, by himself, in an hour, a bishop in three hours, a priest in five and a friar in seven, how long would it take them to pray out three souls from purgatory, all praying together?' Which of these is nearest to the expected answer?

 A 1 h $41\frac{1}{2}$ min   *B* 1 h 46 min   *C* 1 h $47\frac{1}{2}$ min
       D 5 h 20 min   *E* an eternity

COMMENTS AND STATISTICS
1992

Statistics: There were 80 000 entries from 1250 schools. The cut-off scores for the award of certificates this year were as follows:

Gold	≥ **70**	(around 6% of participants)
Silver	≥ **58**	(around 13% of participants)
Bronze	≥ **47**	(around 21% of participants)

The percentage of participants choosing the five options for each question were as follows:

Qn:	1	2	3	4	5	6	7	8	9	10	11	12	13	14	15
A	3.2	4.0	_20.1_	9.4	_51.0_	24.1	3.6	29.0	_15.4_	27.4	6.5	16.9	41.7	40.4	5.6
B	4.4	_80.9_	63.7	_27.6_	8.5	_57.7_	4.2	31.8	1.9	6.4	_17.6_	_48.0_	8.9	29.5	59.4
C	_84.2_	10.9	6.7	42.8	17.7	2.2	3.0	_10.4_	25.3	11.7	13.2	15.6	_35.1_	14.1	8.5
D	2.7	1.3	2.4	17.0	6.5	5.6	5.6	12.7	2.2	_39.5_	13.0	7.7	2.9	4.8	8.5
E	4.2	2.3	5.6	1.9	10.9	8.5	_80.9_	11.1	52.8	8.8	35.9	6.0	9.5	_6.6_	_15.3_
0	0.9	0.4	0.9	0.8	4.7	1.3	2.3	4.6	1.9	4.1	13.1	5.3	1.4	3.9	2.0
2+	0.5	0.3	0.6	0.5	0.6	0.5	0.4	0.5	0.5	2.1	0.6	0.5	0.5	0.8	0.6

Qn:	16	17	18	19	20	21	22	23	24	25
A	26.9	15.0	_39.0_	13.4	10.5	35.7	2.7	_9.8_	21.6	6.6
B	17.2	16.8	8.9	14.4	11.0	14.3	9.5	25.7	14.1	10.0
C	8.0	26.3	10.6	23.5	18.6	_10.6_	32.8	12.1	_16.3_	_10.8_
D	_23.4_	_30.3_	14.1	_19.1_	11.5	7.1	9.7	8.9	11.4	23.0
E	21.3	7.8	7.3	19.5	_36.1_	7.8	_18.1_	14.2	6.3	18.4
0	2.1	2.9	18.9	8.7	11.4	23.7	26.4	28.5	29.5	30.6
2+	1.1	0.9	1.1	1.4	0.9	0.8	0.8	0.8	0.8	0.7

The Problems Group believe they produced an accessible, challenging paper with some really easy 'starters' (**Q1, 2**) and some instructive, elementary (though not 'easy') problems in the middle range (**Q5–12**). The statistics tell a rather different story. Given the ability of those taking part, the success rate in **Q1** should have been nearer 90% (as indeed it was for girls), and that for **Q2** should have been **above** 90%. The responses for **Q3** suggest worryingly that pupils are *rarely expected to handle more than two pieces of information at a time*. **Q4** is more basic and more disturbing (look at the spread of responses).

There is much to learn from these statistics – both local and national – and I hope you will make time to discuss them with your colleagues (especially **Q11**!).

Questions 1–15: 5 marks each

1. The first description of how to use logarithms to do multiplication was published in 1614 by John Napier (Scots, 1550–1617). How many years ago was that?

    A 371   *B* 379   *C* 380   *D* 381   *E* 389

2. If the shading of squares is continued so that m and m' become lines of symmetry of the completed diagram, what is the largest possible number of squares left unshaded?

    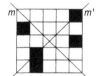

    A 5   *B* 7   *C* 9   *D* 11   *E* 17

3. A race starts at the top of Ben Nevis (1343 m), goes via Scafell Pike (978 m) and ends on top of Snowdon (1085 m). How much further do participants travel down than up?

    A 198 m   *B* 258 m   *C* 365 m   *D* 2321 m   *E* 3406 m

4. Which number is not divisible by 4?

    A 2 345 678   *B* 2468   *C* 123 456   *D* 1248   *E* 8 765 432

5. Some sequences of words, like *Was it a car or a cat I saw?*, read the same both forwards and backwards. Which of these examples is *not* like this?

    A 'E daft sum must fade   *B* Push tame maths up   *C* Poor data droop
          D Times must sums emit   *E* Must he divide the sum?

6. A school has 657 pupils. There are 384 pupils in School Year 9 or above and 376 in School Year 9 or below. How many pupils are there in School Year 9 in this school?

    A 8   *B* 103   *C* 113   *D* 273   *E* 281

7. Which shape *cannot* be filled, without any overlapping, using copies of the tile shown on the right?

    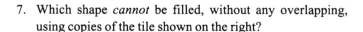

8. My computer screen displays up to eighty characters (letters, figures or spaces) on each line. If there is not enough room for a word or a number at the end of a line, the whole word is moved to start at the beginning of the next line. I type (in figures) the numbers from 1 to 100, with a space after each number. What is the last number to appear on the first line?

    A 26   *B* 27   *C* 28   *D* 29   *E* 30

9. The missing numbers in this calculation add up to

    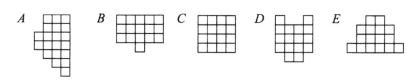

    A 7   *B* 11   *C* 13   *D* 15   *E* 21

10. In 'conker arithmetic' when a '3-er' plays a '4-er' only the winner survives and is then called an '8-er' (since $8 = 3 + 4 + 1$). If five '2-ers' play until only one is left, what will the winner be?

    A 10-er   *B* 11-er   *C* 14-er   *D* 15-er   *E* 17-er

11. In 1742 Christian Goldbach (German, 1690 – 1764) wrote a letter to Leonard Euler (Swiss, 1707 – 83), saying that he believed every even number greater than 2 can be written as the sum of two prime numbers. How many different ways are there of writing the number 42 as the sum of two prime numbers? (Note: 3 + 5 and 5 + 3 would *not* be considered to be different ways of writing the number 8.)

    A 1   *B* 2   *C* 3   *D* 4   *E* more than four

12 *O* is the centre of the circle. Find the size of angle θ.

     A 35°   *B* 45°   *C* 60°   *D* 70°   *E* 90°

13. In 1991 Carl Lewis set a world record of 9.86 seconds for the 100 metre sprint. What was his approximate average speed in miles per hour? (Note: 1 mile is approximately equal to 1600 metres.)

     A 14 mph   *B* 17 mph   *C* 20 mph   *D* 23 mph   *E* 26 mph

14. Gill has now started primary skool and is learning to spell. We got her to help by writing out this queschun for us. We gave her a score of 100 to start with and deducted 10% of her running total each time we found a word spelt rong. What was her final score?

     A 70   *B* 72.9   *C* 80   *D* 81   *E* 90

15. The diagram shows a figure in which all the long sides are the same length and each is twice as long as each of the short sides. The angles are all right angles and the area of the figure is 200 cm². What is the perimeter of the figure?

     A 20 cm   *B* 40 cm   *C* 60 cm   *D* 80 cm   *E* 100 cm

Questions 16–25: 6 marks each

16. *Piffling Pizzas* sell pizzas with diameters 4 inches, 6 inches, 8 inches and 10 inches for £2, £4, £8 and £12 respectively. If the pizzas all have the same thickness, which size will give the most pizza per £1?

     A 4 inch   *B* 6 inch   *C* 8 inch   *D* 10 inch   *E* all the same

17. In a school photo the 630 pupils are arranged in rows. Each row contains three fewer pupils than the row in front of it. What number of rows is *not* possible?

     A 3   *B* 4   *C* 5   *D* 6   *E* 7

18. Sam the super snail is climbing a vertical gravestone 1 metre high. She climbs at a steady speed of 30 cm per hour, but each time the church clock strikes the shock causes her to slip down 1 cm. The clock only strikes the hours, so at 1 o'clock she would slip back 1 cm, at 2 o'clock she would slip back 2 cm and so on. If she starts to climb just after the clock strikes 3 pm, when will she reach the top?

    A 3.50 pm   B 6.20 pm   C 6.50 pm   D 7.04 pm   E 7.20 pm

19. I throw a ball vertically up into the air. Which of these graphs might reasonably show the ball's speed (*s*) against the time (*t*) since leaving my hand?

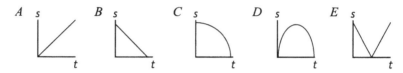

20. I have a microcassette that can be set to run at two speeds, 24 cm per sec or 12 cm per sec. The maximum length of time I can record for is sixty minutes if I use both sides of the tape. How long, in metres, is the tape?

    A 216   B 432   C 1064   D 21 600   E 43 200

21. Only the digits 2, 3, 4, 5, 6, 7 are used in this multiplication, and each letter represents a different digit. What is the value of *M* + *U* + *C* + *K*?

    A 14   B 16   C 17   D 18   E 19

22. I walk at 4 km per hour and run at 6 km per hour. I find I can save 3 minutes and 45 seconds by running instead of walking to school in the mornings. How far do I live from school?

    A 0.125 km   B 0.375 km   C 0.75 km   D 6.9 km   E 7.5 km

23. *PQR* is an equilateral triangle. The points *U*, *V*, *W*, *X*, *Y*, *Z* trisect the sides. What is the ratio of the area of the shaded quadrilateral *UWXY* to the whole triangle *PQR*?

    A 4:9   B 5:9   C 2:5   D 4:5   E 1:2

40   *Sixth UK Schools Mathematical Challenge 1993*

24. How many pears can I buy for £1.08 if seventy almonds cost the same as fifty chestnuts, forty-eight chestnuts cost the same as one pomegranate, eighteen pomegranates cost the same as twenty-eight lemons, ten lemons cost the same as twenty-five pears, and one hundred and eight almonds cost 9p?

    A 12   *B* 75   *C* 108   *D* 358   *E* not a whole number

25. A crossnumber is like a crossword except that the answers are numbers with one digit in each square.

Which odd digit does not appear in the solution to this crossnumber?

CLUES

Across (A)
3. Cube
4. Cube

Down (D)
1. Cube
2. Square
3. Cube

    A 1   *B* 3   *C* 5   *D* 7   *E* 9

COMMENTS AND STATISTICS
1993

Statistics: In its last year in this format the UK SMC attracted 105 000 entries from 1500 schools. The cut-off scores for certificates and the detailed results were as follows:

Gold	≥ **75**	(around 6% of participants)
Silver	≥ **63**	(around 13% of participants)
Bronze	≥ **53**	(around 21% of participants)

The percentage of participants choosing the five options for each question were as follows:

Qn:	1	2	3	4	5	6	7	8	9	10	11	12	13	14	15
A	1.7	13.6	3.5	<u>70.1</u>	3.9	19.6	<u>75.7</u>	6.8	5.8	10.3	9.4	8.0	15.2	61.5	7.3
B	<u>89.2</u>	10.8	<u>61.4</u>	3.7	3.7	<u>53.8</u>	4.9	4.5	19.6	34.3	11.1	8.5	25.2	<u>23.0</u>	10.4
C	1.6	<u>36.6</u>	19.1	12.3	3.5	11.6	7.7	8.3	10.1	<u>31.7</u>	17.8	4.9	14.2	7.7	17.2
D	2.9	25.6	8.3	2.8	3.8	7.1	5.4	18.2	5.7	13.1	<u>21.8</u>	<u>60.2</u>	<u>18.6</u>	2.6	<u>37.6</u>
E	0.1	10.0	4.2	8.3	<u>83.0</u>	3.3	4.5	<u>57.5</u>	<u>55.8</u>	8.2	33.1	14.2	13.3	3.2	17.6
0	0.5	3.2	3.3	2.6	1.5	4.5	1.6	4.5	2.7	2.3	6.5	3.8	13.2	1.7	9.7
2+	0.1	0.2	0.2	0.2	0.5	0.1	0.3	0.3	0.2	0.2	0.2	0.3	0.3	0.2	0.2

Qn:	16	17	18	19	20	21	22	23	24	25
A	48.2	13.6	7.2	12.5	<u>9.2</u>	8.8	8.1	<u>10.1</u>	17.9	8.7
B	<u>10.5</u>	28.0	21.4	8.6	17.3	12.7	17.1	11.1	<u>11.6</u>	<u>9.9</u>
C	8.7	14.1	<u>29.7</u>	11.9	16.5	13.7	<u>22.9</u>	13.6	7.7	15.0
D	10.4	<u>10.8</u>	21.1	36.9	15.5	<u>24.2</u>	11.2	14.7	5.3	16.3
E	14.4	14.4	8.2	<u>17.1</u>	16.3	9.1	4.9	14.6	20.3	11.7
0	7.6	18.9	12.2	12.8	25.0	31.2	35.6	35.6	36.9	38.2
2+	0.2	0.3	0.2	0.3	0.2	0.2	0.2	0.3	0.3	0.2

The Problems Group struggled to produce an accessible, challenging paper with some easy 'starters' (**Q1, 3, 4**!), some elementary problems which require pupils to read (**Q2, 3, 5, 6, 10, 14**), and some problems for pupils to 'do' (**Q2, 7, 9**). UK SMC problems are never easy; but they are not all that difficult. The statistics suggest strongly that thought needs to be given to some very basic questions – such as **Q2, Q3, Q4, Q11** (why 1 is *not* a prime), and **Q16**. It is worth discussing likely explanations for common errors (such as 2D, 3C, 6A, 8D, 9B, 10B, 11E, 12E, 13B, 14A and especially 16A).

We believe strongly that all mathematics requires *interpretation* (**Q10**), and that *reading* and *sifting information* (**Q3, 6**) is an essential part of mathematical problem-solving. Because nothing depends on the outcome, we feel free to include perhaps one problem which is meant to generate discussion (**Q19**?), and one or more which will generate a smile.

ANSWERS TO SECTION A

1988: *E D B A D   E C E C C   E B B A D   A A B D B   C E D A E*

1989: *E C C A A   E B B B A   D D C D A   B C D E C   A E B B D*

1990: *A C E C D   B B B D C   E D E C E   B B D A D   D B E A A*

1991: *A D C A E   D E B E D   D B A D B   D C D C B   E A C B B*

1992: *C B A B A   B E C A D   B B C E E   D D A D E   C E A C C*

1993: *B C B A E   B A E E C   D D D B D   B D C E A   D C A B B*

Section B

Short Problem Papers

There is nothing so wrong ... as believing the answer!

Richard Feynman

INTRODUCTION TO SECTION B

Section B contains mini-problem-papers in the same style as those in Section A. Each mini-paper contains ten questions and should be suitable for a 30 minute time-slot – either in class, or for homework. This does not mean, however, that the problems are easy. They are not. Students should not expect easy success, but must be prepared to think carefully, and then to learn from their mistakes.

Each year the 25 questions on the Challenge paper are chosen from a completely fresh set of around 150 problems. Many of these are excellent questions, but they cannot all be used. Some get left out purely by chance. Others raise important mathematical ideas, but do so in a way which demands discussion – something we cannot arrange in a large national event. Section B contains the best of these questions in a convenient and usable form. As with the annual Challenge paper, the questions here are intended to make pupils *think*, and then learn from their mistakes. So please discourage guessing, and make time to discuss the problems and solutions (and mistakes!) with your pupils.

The problems may be short, but they are surprisingly rich, and there is much that warrants discussion. Even where pupils choose the right option it is worth exploring alternative approaches. For example, faced with the question (Paper 1, Question 9):

> *At which of these times is the angle between*
> *the two hands of a clock exactly 170°?*

one could (a) try each of the five options in turn, combining accurate drawing and estimation; or (b) calculate the hard way (each minute the minute hand moves so much, while the hour hand moves so much, so the angle between the two hands increases/decreases by exactly so many degrees each minute, etc.); or (c) observe that 170° is exactly 10° short of 180°, so we want the hands to be almost opposite each other; and the hour hand moves 10° in exactly so many minutes, so we want the minute hand on 4 or 8. There is mileage here for all abilities and all ages. By not providing solutions we leave you the pleasure of extracting the treasure from this veritable treasure trove.

We repeat what we observed in the Preface. Teachers will use these problems in their own way. Teaching styles vary, and different teachers have different ways of motivating their pupils, or of introducing new topics. Nevertheless most teaching and learning in mathematics involves two clearly distinct stages.

- Pupils must first understand and master some simple technique. This will often be introduced in a standard way, and then practised via a sequence of routine questions, phrased in easily recognisable language – language which is chosen to evoke a standard response.

But when pupils come to *use* the mathematics they know, they have to work *outside* the relevant chapter of the textbook – with its give-away title ('Place value', 'Angles', or whatever) and its familiar, predictable, highly suggestive language.

- Pupils therefore need to master the much more elusive skill of *making mathematical sense* of simple problems in the absence of give-away clues. They must learn to *interpret* the problems as stated, *decide* what has to be done, and *select* the relevant techniques to achieve this.

This important second stage requires regular exposure to sets of *short* problems which force pupils to think, and which cannot be solved by merely recognising key words and then applying standard tricks.

Thus, whereas the first stage involves *one-step* routine questions, in which pupils practise a standard technique, the second stage requires that pupils be regularly confronted with simple two-step (or multi-step) problems which cannot be solved by blindly applying the relevant routine method.

Ideally these two 'stages' should blend together, with the first ten routine questions on a new topic including at least one 'less routine' problem, the next ten questions including (say) three 'less routine' problems, and so on.

None of the problems in this section are routine. They all require students to select appropriate methods, to sift information, and to combine two or more steps. The problems are nevertheless *succinct*. In seeking to stimulate young minds, nothing is gained, and much tends to be lost, by too much extraneous 'noise'. Where a context is used, it is more likely to draw on, and appeal to, students' *imagination* than to pay lip-service to the 'real world'. Despite this, there are plenty of problems which link mathematics to the world around us.

Finally I should perhaps stress that, though the problems have a serious educational purpose, *they are also meant to be fun.* In mathematics, as in sport or in music, satisfaction comes from the challenge of confronting opposition that is tough, but not too tough: in other words, from tackling good problems.

1.   The papers in Section B are aimed at pupils aged 11–15 (School Years 7–10 English style).

2.   Each mini-paper contains 10 questions.

3.   Each mini-paper should fill a 30-minute class or homework slot.

4.   The papers are roughly graded: early questions on each paper, and earlier papers in Section B, tend to be easier, while later questions on each paper, and later papers in the section, tend to be more demanding.

5.   The problems are meant to be done **without a calculator**.

A brief discussion of the background philosophy (in particular, the reason why the problems are meant to be tackled without a calculator) may be found in the introduction to Section A.

PAPER 1

1. What is the value of $((1 \times 2 \div (3 \times 4) - 5) \times 6 - 7) \div (8 \times 9)$?

   $A \ -\frac{1}{2}$ $B \ -\frac{189}{8}$ $C \ -\frac{7}{24}$ $D \ -\frac{1}{72}$ E none of these

2. A diagonal of a polygon is a straight line joining any two non-adjacent corners. A decagon has ten corners. How many diagonals does it have?

   A 35 B 40 C 45 D 60 E 70

3. 1990 is exactly ten times a prime number. When will be the next year which is exactly ten times a prime number?

   A 2210 B 2190 C 2170 D 2130 E 2110

4. Einstein (E), Newton (N) and Pythagoras (P) are all dead now. Suppose they were all still alive. Who would be oldest and who would be youngest? (Arrange them in order of age: oldest first, youngest last.)

   A EPN B NEP C NPE D PEN E PNE

5. Four of the answers to this question represent the same fraction. Which is the odd one out?

   A 0.4 $B \ \frac{1}{3}+\frac{1}{15}$ $C \ \frac{2}{5}$ D 40% $E \ \frac{1}{2}+\frac{3}{8}$

6. A 3 cm by 3 cm by 3 cm cube is painted all over its outside and is then cut into 27 smaller cubes. How many of these smaller cubes have paint on more than one face?

   A 14 B 18 C 20 D 22 E 24

7. You roll two dice, each with two red, two blue and two white faces. What is the probability that both dice show matching colours?

   $A \ \frac{1}{216}$ $B \ \frac{1}{108}$ $C \ \frac{1}{36}$ $D \ \frac{1}{12}$ $E \ \frac{1}{3}$

8. An icosahedron is a regular polyhedron with twenty triangular faces. How many edges does it have?

    A 12   *B* 20   *C* 24   *D* 30   *E* 60

9. At which of these times is the angle between the two hands of a clock exactly 170°?

    A 3.50   *B* 5.00   *C* 6.30   *D* 8.10   *E* 10.20

10. Rowntosh-Mackintree make Easter eggs. Each egg contains six toffees, the toffees being selected from three different sorts. How many different selections are possible if each egg must contain at least one toffee of each sort?

    A 3   *B* 6   *C* 9   *D* 10   *E* 18

PAPER 2

1. What is one-third of 299?

    A 33 B $99\frac{1}{3}$ C $99\frac{2}{3}$ D $100\frac{2}{3}$ E 897

2. For which of these shapes are the diagonals the only axes of symmetry?

    A square B rectangle C rhombus
    D regular hexagon E regular octagon

3. To the nearest whole number, what is the mean number of letters per word in this sentence?

    A 2 B 3 C 4 D 5 E 17

4. The 21st century will begin on 1 January 2001. What day of the week will that be?

    A Friday B Saturday C Sunday D Monday E Tuesday

5. In some years an extra second is added on to 31 December to keep the clocks in time with the rotation of the earth. How many seconds does 31 December have when this happens?

    A 1441 B 3601 C 8641 D 14401 E 86401

6. What is the area of a circle with circumference C?

    A πC B πC^2 C $\frac{C^2}{4}$ D $\frac{C^2}{4\pi}$ E $\frac{C^2}{4\pi^2}$

7. If I write all the whole numbers from 1 to 500 in a row, what will be the 1000th digit that I write?

    A 0 B 1 C 3 D 6 E 7

8. The average of x and y is $\dfrac{3y}{4}$. What is $\dfrac{x}{y}$?

$A\ \frac{1}{4}$ $\qquad B\ \frac{1}{2}$ $\qquad C\ \frac{3}{4}$ $\qquad D\ 2$ $\qquad E\ $ can't be sure

9. Imagine a bridge 2.5 km long which is fixed only at its ends. During the summer heat it expands lengthwise by just one metre (that is, less than half a millimetre per metre). As a result the bridge bulges upwards slightly. By roughly how much would you expect the centre of the bridge to rise?

$A\ 0.5\,\text{m}$ $\qquad B\ 1\,\text{m}$ $\qquad C\ 2.5\,\text{m}$ $\qquad D\ 5\,\text{m}$ $\qquad E\ 35\,\text{m}$

10. The sides of a rectangle are measured as 8 cm and 10 cm, to the nearest cm in each case. What is the greatest possible value of the rectangle's area, to the nearest cm^2?

$A\ 80$ $\qquad B\ 82$ $\qquad C\ 84$ $\qquad D\ 85$ $\qquad E\ 89$

PAPER 3

1. In 1990, 1 February fell on a Thursday. On what day of the week did April Fools' Day fall that year?

    A Sunday   *B* Monday   *C* Wednesday   *D* Thursday   *E* Friday

2. Which of these numbers is the smallest?

    A $\frac{1}{3}$ *B* $\frac{3}{10}$ *C* $\frac{333}{1000}$ *D* $\frac{7}{20}$ *E* 0.33

3. A 4 by 4 square has its area numerically equal to its perimeter. Which of the following sized rectangles has a similar property?

    A 3 by 4   *B* 3 by 5   *C* 3.5 by 6   *D* 2.5 by 10   *E* 2 by 2

4. As a regular customer in my favourite restaurant I get a 10% discount. But to the cost of the meal must be added 17.5% VAT and 12% service charge. If the percentages are to be worked out in turn (with each percentage – addition or discount – being based on the previous answer), which order of working leaves me the least to pay?

    A VAT, service, discount   *B* service, VAT, discount   *C* discount, VAT, service
    D discount, service, VAT   *E* it makes no difference

5. I start with a square, increase one side by 3 cm and decrease an adjacent side by 2 cm to form a rectangle of area 24 cm². Find the perimeter of the rectangle (in cm).

    A 20   *B* 22   *C* 24   *D* 28   *E* 30

6. In a science lab, Amy, Bea, Cyn, Dee and Eve measured a metal bar using the same measuring instrument, but each read the scale to a different level of accuracy. Their five answers are shown below. Four of them are correct (to the chosen level of accuracy), but one is not. Which is the odd one out?

   A 240 mm B 243 mm C 243.7 mm D 243.69 mm E 243.692 mm

7. A quiz has 25 questions with four points awarded for each correct answer and one point deducted for each incorrect answer, with zero for each question omitted. John scores 77 points. How many questions did he omit?

   A 1 B 2 C 3 D 5 E can't be sure

8. The expression $n^2 - n + 11$ gives a prime number for all but one of these values of n. Which is the odd one out?

   A $n = 2$ B $n = 3$ C $n = 5$ D $n = 7$ E $n = 11$

9. How many pounds worth of (ordinary sized) first-class stamps would be needed to cover one side of an A4 sheet of paper, leaving no gaps?

   A £5 B £20 C £30 D £50 E £65

10. A taut wire of length w emits a single note when plucked. If it were half as long it would emit the same note but one octave *higher*. How long should the same wire be to emit the same note but one octave *lower*?

   A $(1.5) \times w$ B $\sqrt{2} \times w$ C $2 \times w$ D $3 \times w$ E $4 \times w$

PAPER 4

1. Which gives the biggest answer?

    A 2.3×8 B 3.4×7 C 4.5×6 D 5.6×5 E 6.7×4

2. The iceman found recently in a glacier on the border between Italy and Austria was at first thought to be about 5300 years old. Roughly when did he have his 14th birthday?

    A 2700 BC B 3300 BC C 3700 BC D 5300 BC E 7300 BC

3. In the diagram $ABCD$ is a square. $AB = BC = 2$ m, and $DE = DF = 1$ m. Find the area in m^2 of $\triangle BEF$.

    A $\frac{1}{2}\sqrt{10}$ B $\sqrt{10}$ C $1\frac{1}{2}$ D 2 E $2\frac{1}{2}$

4. How many of statements (i) – (iv) are false?
   (i) A cube has six faces.
   (ii) A cube has eight corners.
   (iii) A cube has twelve edges.
   (iv) A cube has thirteen axes of rotational symmetry.

    A none B one C two D three E four

5. In a set of number rods, there is one rod of length 10, two rods of length 9, three of length 8, and so on. If all these rods were laid end to end in one line, how long would the line be?

    A 55 B 100 C 110 D 220 E 385

6. I have lots of 5p and 11p stamps. What is the largest amount I cannot make up using just these two types of stamp?

    A 17p B 39p C 43p D 48p E 53p

7. Giuseppe the clockmaker has two antique clocks. One gains ten seconds every hour, while the other loses twenty seconds every hour. He set both clocks to show the correct time at 9 am on 4 February 1993. On what date will they next show the correct time simultaneously?

A 19 February   *B* 6 March   *C* 5 April   *D* 4 June   *E* 3 August

8. In the number 0.123451234512345 ... (recurring) what is the 1992th digit after the decimal point?

A 1   *B* 2   *C* 3   *D* 4   *E* 5

9. Roughly how many million seconds have you been alive?

A 4   *B* 40   *C* 400   *D* 4000   *E* 40 000

10. In Morse code each letter is replaced by a sequence of dots and dashes. How many ordinary English words (excluding proper names) are there whose Morse code consists entirely of dots, or entirely of dashes?

A 3   *B* 4   *C* 5   *D* 6   *E* more than 6

PAPER 5

1. Amita has twice as much money as Bill, and Cathy has half as much again as Amita has. If Cathy has 20p less than Drusia has and Drusia has £2, how much money does Bill have?

    A 30p *B* 60p *C* 80p *D* £1.20 *E* £1.80

2. How many parallelograms are there in this figure?

    A 0   *B* 4   *C* 8   *D* 9   *E* 15

3. How many different four-figure numbers can be made using the digits 1, 9, 9, 1?

    A 4   *B* 6   *C* 12   *D* 16   *E* 24

4. Which of these numbers is *not* equivalent to 66%?

    A $\frac{66}{100}$ *B* 0.66   *C* $\frac{33}{50}$ *D* $\frac{2}{3}$ *E* $\frac{198}{300}$

5. When Tessa and Fatima run a 100 metre race, Tessa wins by 10 m. They then repeat the race, this time with Tessa starting 11 m behind the starting line. If both girls run at the same speed as before, what would be the expected result?

    A Tessa wins by 1 m   *B* Tessa just wins   *C* a dead heat
    D Fatima just wins   *E* Fatima wins by 1 m

6. A ream of A4 paper contains 500 sheets and is 4.7 cm thick. How thick is a single sheet?

    A about 100 mm   *B* a bit more than 1 mm   *C* a bit less than 1 mm
    D a bit more than 0.1 mm   *E* a bit less than 0.1 mm

7. This figure is made up entirely of arcs of circles of diameter 2 cm. What is its perimeter (in cm)?

    A 2π   *B* 4π   *C* 6π   *D* 8π   *E* 12π

8. Sound travels at about 330 metres per second, but light travels so much faster that it arrives almost instantaneously. How long a gap do you expect between seeing the flash and hearing the thunder from a storm 4 km away?

    A $\frac{1}{3}$ s   *B* $1\frac{1}{3}$ s   *C* 3 s   *D* 6 s   *E* 12 s

9. Six volumes of an encyclopedia, each volume 4 cm thick, are on a library shelf in the order: Vol. 1, Vol. 2, Vol. 3, Vol. 4, Vol. 5, Vol. 6 from left to right. A bookworm starts outside the front cover of Volume 1 and eats his way by the shortest route through to the back cover of Volume 4. How far does the bookworm travel?

    A 4 cm   *B* 8 cm   *C* 12 cm   *D* 16 cm   *E* 24 cm

10. On what day of the week does Christmas Day fall in the year 2000?

    A Sunday   *B* Monday   *C* Tuesday   *D* Wednesday   *E* Thursday

PAPER 6

1. What is the difference between nine hundred and ninety-nine thousand and 990 001?

    A 1   *B* 899   *C* 901   *D* 8999   *E* 9001

2. If today is Thursday, what day will it be in 100 days' time?

    A Friday   *B* Saturday   *C* Sunday   *D* Monday   *E* Tuesday

3. When you reverse the digits of the number 13, the number increases by 18. How many other two-digit numbers increase by 18 when their digits are reversed?

    A 0   *B* 2   *C* 4   *D* 5   *E* 6

4. The owl and the pussycat went to see if the piggy would sell his ring. The owl asked *'Little pig, are you willing/ To sell for one shilling/ Your ring?' Said the piggy, 'I will'*. They had plenty of money – old pennies, old threepenny bits, and old sixpences. In how many different ways could they pay for the ring? (One old shilling was the same as twelve old pennies.)

    A 3   *B* 7   *C* 8   *D* 9   *E* 12

5. Which of these shapes has the largest area?

6. On the London Underground railway system, the Circle Line forms a continuous loop with twenty-seven stations on it. Suppose the underground trains start at 5.30 am and run until midnight. The average time taken between stations (including stops) is about $2\frac{1}{2}$ minutes. If a train ran all day without going out of service, approximately how many circuits of the Circle Line would you expect it to make?

   A $2\frac{1}{2}$ *B* 16   *C* $18\frac{1}{2}$ *D* 24   *E* 27

7. *ABCD* is a parallelogram. What is the length *x*?

   A 4   *B* 7   *C* 8   *D* 10   *E* can't be sure

8. In this multiplication *U*, *K*, *S*, *M*, *C* represent different digits. What number does *S* represent?

   A 2   *B* 4   *C* 6   *D* 7   *E* 9

$$\begin{array}{r} UKSMC \\ \times \quad 4 \\ \hline CMSKU \end{array}$$

9. If *x* men take *y* days to build *z* houses, how many days would *q* men take to build *r* houses?

   A $\dfrac{qry}{xz}$ *B* $\dfrac{ryz}{qx}$ *C* $\dfrac{qz}{rxy}$ *D* $\dfrac{xyr}{qz}$ *E* $\dfrac{rz}{qxy}$

10. A squeezable toothpaste tube is originally in the form of a cylinder 12 cm long, with diameter 4 cm. The short cylindrical nozzle has diameter 5 mm. What length of toothpaste can the tube produce?

    A 9.6 cm   *B* 12 cm   *C* 16 cm   *D* 96 cm   *E* 768 cm

PAPER 7

1. Which number is halfway between 179 and 837?

    A 453   B 458   C 503   D 508   E 509

2. In a 4 by 4 magic square the sum of the four entries in each row, in each column, and in each of the two main diagonals are all the same. When the magic square shown here is completed, what is the sum of the two entries marked ∗?

		7	12
∗	4	9	
10	5		3
8	11		∗

    A 19   B 21   C 28   D 30   E 31

3. One of these numbers is equal to the product of the other four. Which is it?

    A −2   B $\frac{3}{4}$ C $\frac{1}{6}$ D $-\frac{1}{4}$ E 9

4. Which of the following has the greatest perimeter?

    A   a square of side 3 cm
    B   a circle of diameter 4 cm
    C   a right-angled triangle with shorter sides of lengths 3 cm and 4 cm
    D   a rectangle with area 16 cm²
    E   an equilateral triangle with side $4\frac{1}{2}$ cm

5. If you write **S M C** on a sheet of card and hold the card upside down in front of a mirror, what would you see in the mirror?

    A ƆMƧ   B ƧMƆ   C SWƆ   D ƆWS   E ƧWƆ

6. The normal selling price of an article is cut by 20% in a sale. This reduces the trader's profit on the price she paid for it to 4%. What percentage profit (to the nearest whole per cent) did she make at the normal selling price?

    A 16   B 24   C 25   D 30   E 84

7. When the cathedral clock strikes four, it takes 8 seconds between the first and last strokes. How many seconds does it take to strike twelve?

   A $18\frac{1}{3}$ B 22 C 24 D $29\frac{1}{3}$ E 32

8. Two numbers have product 36 and sum 20. What is the sum of their squares?

   A 72 B 97 C 153 D 328 E can't be sure

9. Julius Pompous leaves Rome (R) to conquer the five tribes U, K, S, M, C and return home triumphant. The diagram shows the distances (in km) between tribes. What is the least distance (in km) he needs to march?

   A 300 B 310 C 330 D 340 E 350

10. The four-digit number 1 2 ∗ 6 is a perfect square. The value of the digit represented by ∗ is

   A 1 B 3 C 5 D 7 E 9

PAPER 8

1. The largest prime factor of 2310 is

   A 3   *B* 5   *C* 7   *D* 11   *E* 231

2. A farmer had 200 sheep. Eighty died, and all but 25% of those remaining ran away. How many were left?

   A 20   *B* 25   *C* 30   *D* 90   *E* 120

3. The circle centre O has radius 5 cm. A point P is chosen at random inside this circle. What is the probability that P is inside the shaded circle?

   A $\frac{1}{2}$ *B* $\frac{1}{3}$ *C* $\frac{1}{4}$ *D* $\frac{1}{5}$ *E* $\frac{2}{5}$

4. What is the difference between the sum of *all* the odd numbers up to 1992 and the sum of *all* the even numbers up to 1992?

   A 0   *B* 995   *C* 996   *D* 1991   *E* 1992

5. Andrea, Brian and Claire spent an afternoon picking strawberries. Andrea picked 3 kg more than Brian but 2 kg less than Claire. If Brian picked three-quarters of the amount that Claire picked, how much did the three friends pick in total?

   A 5 kg   *B* 15 kg   *C* 20 kg   *D* 35 kg   *E* 53 kg

6. I was one of the thousands of people who stood in the rain in Hyde Park to listen to Luciano Pavarotti's concert in July 1991. On the drive home I heard on the radio that the concert had been broadcast live in Italy. This meant that Pavarotti's rain-soaked voice took twenty times as long to reach me standing in Hyde Park as it did to reach listeners in Italy 1500 km away! If radio waves travel at 3×10^8 ms^{-1} and sound waves at 340 ms^{-1}, how far away from the great tenor was I standing?

   A 17 m   *B* 34 m   *C* 170 m   *D* 340 m   *E* 30 000 km

7. On Old MacDonald's Farm the cows and ducks are singing in full chorus – fifty-four voices and one hundred and seventy stamping feet. If every duck is on a cow and each cow has at most one duck on its back, how many cows are duckless?

    A 0   *B* 8   *C* 10   *D* 31   *E* 54

8. Which gives the biggest answer?

    A   divide 2 by $\frac{1}{2}$
    B   multiply $\frac{1}{2}$ by 2 and add 3
    C   divide $\frac{1}{2}$ by $\frac{1}{4}$ and double the answer
    D   multiply 3 by $\frac{1}{2}$ and divide the answer by $\frac{1}{3}$
    E   divide $\frac{2}{3}$ by $\frac{1}{2}$ and double the answer

9. Suppose you spent New Year's Day driving once (anticlockwise) around London on the M25. Roughly how much further would the car's outer wheel travel than the inner wheel?

    A 1 m   *B* 10 m   *C* 100 m   *D* 1 km   *E* 10 km

10. The fraction $\dfrac{n}{1992}$ has a decimal which terminates. What is the smallest possible value of n?

    A 1   *B* 3   *C* 83   *D* 249   *E* 1992

PAPER 9

1. What is the value of $19 \times (9 - 0) - (199 + 0) + 19 + 90 \div (1 \times 9 + 9 \times 0)$?

    A 1   B 6   C $10\frac{1}{9}$ D 11   E 1990

2. The sides of a triangle have lengths of $7\frac{1}{2}$ cm, 11 cm and x cm, where x is a whole number. What is the smallest possible value of x?

    A 1   B 2   C 3   D 4   E 5

3. In the division $24\,874 \div 17$, which digits should one change in the first number to increase the answer by 100?

    A first only   B first and second   C second and third
              D third only   E first, second and third

4. In my class of no more than 40 pupils there are exactly 10% more girls than boys. How many girls are there?

    A 10   B 11   C 18   D 20   E 21

5. Which of these whole numbers is closest to the square root of 1990?

    A 44   B 45   C 498   D 995   E 3 960 100

6. If I write one digit per second, how long will it take me to write out all the numbers from 1 to 1989?

    A 33 min 9 s   B 1 h 22 min 39 s   C 1 h 54 min
              D 1 h 54 min 9 s   E 2 h 12 min 9 s

7. A man has 720 sheep. He shears half of them on Thursday and two-thirds of the remainder on Friday. How many are left to be sheared on Saturday?

    A 120   B 240   C 288   D 600   E $718\frac{5}{6}$

8. *PQRST* is a regular pentagon. *U* is the reflection of *R* in *QS*. How big is ∠ *UST*?

    A 18°   *B* 36°   *C* 48°   *D* 54°   *E* 72°

9. You have to arrange four different square numbers, each with three digits, in the two rows (top and bottom) and two columns (left and right), but the digit in the bottom right corner must be 0. (One solution is shown.) Each solution can be reflected in the dotted line to give another solution, so solutions come in pairs. How many pairs of solutions are there altogether?

1	4	4
2	■	0
1	0	0

    A 2   *B* 3   *C* 4   *D* 5   *E* 6

10. A solid metal sphere of radius 32 cm is melted down and recast to make 64 identical small spheres. What will be the radius of each small sphere?

    A $\frac{1}{2}$ cm   *B* 1 cm   *C* 2 cm   *D* 4 cm   *E* 8 cm

PAPER 10

1. 1992 equals

   A $8 \times 3 + 83$ B $83 \times 8 \times 3$ C 38×83 D $(3 + 83) \times 8$ E 83×83

2. Mars® bars weigh 62.5 g. How many bars have a total weight of 10 kg?

   A 6.25 B 16 C 62.5 D 160 E 625

3. In the triangle PQR the largest angle is 85°. To the nearest degree, what is the smallest possible size of the smallest angle?

   A 0° B 1° C 5° D 10° E 48°

4. An anagram is a word, or group of words, which uses exactly the same letters as some other familiar word. Thus *NILE* is an anagram of *LINE*, and *A GRANMA* is an anagram of *ANAGRAM*. All five of the following are anagrams of things in geometry, but one is not a geometrical object. Which is the odd one out?

   A *GLEAN* B *PENAL* C *RUSH MOB*
         D *OPEN GNAT* E *GRASPY OATH*

5. How big is the angle marked x?

   A 40° B 80° C 100° D 120° E 140°

   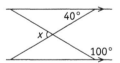

6. 24 000 runners completed the 1991 New York Marathon. Their average time for the run was approximately 3 hours and 40 minutes. If the second runner had not been allowed to start until the first runner had finished, the third runner was not allowed to start until the second runner had finished, and so on, in what year would the race have finished?

   A 1998 B 1999 C 2001 D 2005 E 2009

7. I want to cut this cuboid into pieces which are all identical and exactly similar in shape to the original cuboid. What is the smallest possible number of pieces?

    A 2   *B* 3   *C* 4   *D* 6   *E* 8

8. I write out all the whole numbers, starting from 1. If I wrote 1994 digits altogether, what was the last complete number I wrote down?

    A 664   *B* 699   *C* 700   *D* 701   *E* 1994

9. How many minutes is it to six o'clock if fifty minutes ago it was four times as many minutes past three o'clock?

    A $2\frac{1}{2}$ *B* 26   *C* $32\frac{1}{2}$ *D* 50   *E* $62\frac{1}{2}$

10. (*The Abbot of Canterbury's Puzzle: AD 735–804*)
'One hundred bushels of corn were distributed among one hundred people in such a way that each man received three bushels, each woman two bushels, and each child half a bushel. Given that there are five times as many women as men, how many children are there?'

    A 5   *B* 25   *C* 50   *D* 70   *E* 80

PAPER 11

1. How many times bigger is the '4' than the '8' in 47.8?

    A 0.5   *B* 2   *C* 5   *D* 20   *E* 50

2. Diana has plenty of 18p, 13p and 10p stamps, but no others. Which of the following amounts can she *not* make up exactly?

    A 55p   *B* 64p   *C* 92p   *D* 26p   *E* 85p

3. What is the total surface area (in square units) of this open-topped box?

    A 159   *B* 255   *C* 259   *D* 304   *E* 510

4. Two consecutive numbers add to 71. What is their product?

    A 930   *B* 1190   *C* 1260   *D* 1296   *E* 1332

5. Jim's grandma gives him 36 foreign stamps to start his collection. He collects twelve more each week. How many weeks will it take for his collection to grow to 216 stamps?

    A 15   *B* 18   *C* 21   *D* 24   *E* 180

6. This shape is to be made into a design that has a three-fold symmetry about the dot. When completed the pattern will look like:

    A   *B*   *C*   *D*   *E*

7. Which of the following could *not* be the lengths (in cm) of the three sides of a right-angled triangle?

    A 5, 12, 13   *B* 6, 18, 19   *C* 7, 24, 25   *D* 8, 15, 17   *E* 9, 40, 41

8. If a straight line is drawn across this figure, what is the largest possible number of crossing points one can produce?

    A 6   *B* 8   *C* 10   *D* 11   *E* 15

9. *PQRSTU* is a regular hexagon. *V* is the intersection of *PT* and *SU*. How big is angle *TVS*?

    A 30°   *B* 45°   *C* 60°   *D* 90°   *E* 120°

10. 400 is a three-digit square number that makes a *one*-digit square number when its digits are reversed. How many three-digit squares are there which make *three*-digit squares when their digits are reversed?

    A 1   *B* 2   *C* 6   *D* 7   *E* 8

PAPER 12

1. Four of these expressions have the answers $1, 9, 9, 3$. Which is the odd one out?

    $A \ 1 \times \sqrt{9} \times 9 \div 3$ $B \ 1 \times 9 - (9 - 3)$ $C \ 1 \times 9 \div (\sqrt{9} \times 3)$
    $D \ 1 + \sqrt{9} - \sqrt{9} \times 3$ $E \ 1 \times (9 - \sqrt{9}) + 3$

2. The average number of pupils entered for the UK JMC by the five schools in Mathtown is 70. If four of the schools pay for the minimum entry of 20, how many pupils does the fifth school enter?

    A 60 B 70 C 90 D 120 E 270

3. I have five coins in my pocket, no two with the same value. What is the largest amount of money I could have?

    A £1.65 B £1.85 C £1.87 D £3.20 E £5

4. In a bag there are six white balls and four black balls. I take out two balls at random, one at a time, without replacement. What is the probability that the *second* ball I take is black?

    $A \ \frac{2}{5}$ $B \ \frac{4}{9}$ $C \ \frac{2}{3}$ $D \ \frac{1}{3}$ $E \ \frac{1}{2}$

5. Trace a path from IN to OUT moving through unshaded squares. You may move horizontally or vertically and may not enter any square twice. If you add up your score as you thread your way through, the highest possible score is

    A 250 B 280 C 290 D 310 E 325

6. Which angle could *not* be the interior angle of a regular polygon?

   A 171°   *B* 173°   *C* 175°   *D* 177°   *E* 179°

7. When it is 9 am in London it is 1 am on the same day in Los Angeles and 10 pm on the same day in Auckland, New Zealand. An aeroplane leaves Auckland at 8 pm on a Thursday and takes eighteen hours to fly to Los Angeles. What is the time in Los Angeles when it arrives?

   A 2 pm on Thursday   *B* 5 pm on Thursday   *C* 2 am on Friday
   D 2 pm on Friday   *E* 5 pm on Friday

8. All four interior angles of a parallelogram which is not a rectangle are bisected. What shape is always enclosed by the four bisectors?

   A square
   B rectangle
   C parallelogram which is not a rectangle
   D kite
   E can't be sure

9. By cutting a square out of each corner of a sheet of card (30 cm by 21 cm) and folding up the sides, I can make an open box with a capacity of 1080 cm³. What is the area (in cm²) of each of the squares I have to cut out?

   A 4   *B* 9   *C* 16   *D* 25   *E* 26

10. The number 10^{100} is sometimes called a *googol*. Which of the following is roughly equal to a googol?

   A the number of seconds since the Earth was formed
   B the number of grains of sand on Blackpool beach
   C the number of molecules in the Earth's atmosphere
   D the number of different proper fractions
   E the number of ways 70 children can be arranged in a line

PAPER 13

1. Express the fraction $\frac{1221}{333}$ in its lowest terms.

   $A \ \frac{1221}{333}$ $B \ \frac{407}{111}$ $C \ \frac{136}{37}$ $D \ \frac{111}{33}$ $E \ \frac{11}{3}$

2. The largest prime factor of 1995 is

   $A \ 3$ $B \ 5$ $C \ 7$ $D \ 13$ $E \ 19$

3. I want to type *UK SCHOOLS MATHEMATICAL CHALLENGE* at the top of a page which has room for 90 characters (including spaces) from edge to edge. If I decide to leave two spaces between each 'word', how many spaces should I leave on the left before typing 'U' to make sure the heading lands up in the centre of the page?

   $A \ 25$ $B \ 27$ $C \ 28.5$ $D \ 30$ $E \ 54$

4. If x divided by y is $\frac{4}{5}$ and y divided by z is $\frac{3}{10}$, what is x divided by z?

   $A \ \frac{6}{25}$ $B \ \frac{8}{3}$ $C \ \frac{7}{15}$ $D \ \frac{25}{6}$ $E \ \frac{3}{8}$

5. In the land of Yookayessemcy the currency is based on the *Frac*. 10 *Decs* make 1 *Mult*, and 100 *Mults* make 1 *Frac*. 10 *Fracs* are also called a *Kwid*. How many *Kwids* make 100 *Decs*?

   $A \ 0.001$ $B \ 0.01$ $C \ 0.1$ $D \ 1$ $E \ 10$

6. How many different triangles can be formed by joining up three of these dots?

   $A \ 12$ $B \ 24$ $C \ 32$ $D \ 48$ E none of these

7. The rectangular block shown has total surface area 290 cm². What is *h* (in cm)?

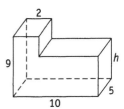

A 4   *B* 5   *C* 6   *D* 7   *E* 8

8. If $a * b$ is the highest common factor of a and b (where a and b are positive whole numbers), which of the following is *not* always true?

    A $a * 1 = 1$ *B* $a * a = a$ *C* $a * b = b * a$
      D $a * (b * c) = (a * b) * c$ *E* $a * (b + c) = a * b + a * c$

9. A small circle just fits inside a semicircle. What is the ratio of the area of the small circle to the area of the shaded region?

    A 2:3   *B* 1:1   *C* 1:2   *D* 3:4   *E* 2:π

10. A room is 10 m square and 4 m high. A spider is in one of the corners on the floor and sees a fly across the room at the diagonally opposite corner on the ceiling. If the fly does not move, what is the shortest distance (in metres) the spider must travel to catch the fly?

    A $\sqrt{216}$ *B* $4 + \sqrt{200}$ *C* 24   *D* $\sqrt{296}$ *E* $\sqrt{416}$

PAPER 14

1. I think of a whole number between one and twenty, square it, add 10, square the answer, then multiply by 2. What can you tell me about the units digit of my final answer?

   A always 0   *B* always 2   *C* always 0 or 2
        D could be any even number   *E* can't be sure

2. My watch gains four minutes every hour. I put it right when I get up at 7 am. What time does my watch show when school ends at 3.45 pm?

   A 3.10   *B* 3.13   *C* 4.00   *D* 4.17   *E* 4.20

3. $\dfrac{\frac{3}{4}+\frac{4}{3}}{5}$ equals

   A $\frac{7}{35}$ *B* $\frac{5}{12}$ *C* $\frac{35}{7}$ *D* $\frac{1}{5}$ *E* $\frac{2}{5}$

4. In how many different orders can four children be arranged in a line if John and Julie refuse to stand next to one another?

   A 4   *B* 6   *C* 12   *D* 16   *E* 24

5. How many squares can be drawn with all four corners on dots in this square grid?

   A 4   *B* 5   *C* 6   *D* 7   *E* more than 7

6. If I write all the whole numbers from 1 to 500 in a row, how many digits will there be?

   A 500   *B* 1387   *C* 1389   *D* 1392   *E* 1395

7. Which of the following is *not* equivalent to 0.000 000 25?

   A 2.5×10^{-7} B $2\frac{1}{2} \times 10^{-7}$ C 250×10^{-9} D $\frac{1}{4} \times 10^{-6}$ E $\frac{1}{4} \times 10^{-7}$

8. A factory employs three hundred and twenty men, three-quarters of whom are married. Three-quarters of the married men have at least one child and three-quarters of these fathers have more than one child. How many have exactly one child?

   A 45 B 135 C 180 D 240 E 320

9. If different letters stand for different digits and $R = 4$, what is the value of $U + K + S + M + C$?

   A 17 B 23 C 26 D 30 E can't be sure

10. *ABCDE* is a regular pentagon. *P* is a point inside the pentagon such that triangle *ABP* is equilateral. How big is angle *DPE*?

    A 42° B 54° C 60° D 84° E 126°

PAPER 15

1. Given that $15 \times 172 = 2580$, what is 0.15×1.72 equal to?

   A 258   *B* 25.8   *C* 2.58   *D* 0.258   *E* 0.0258

2. How many triangles (of all shapes and sizes) can be found in the diagram on the right?

   A 5   *B* 6   *C* 9   *D* 10   *E* 11

   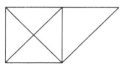

3. $2 \times 2 \times 2 \times 2 \times 2 \times 2 \times 5 \times 5 \times 5 \times 5 \times 5$ equals

   A 37   *B* 89   *C* 100 000   *D* 200 000   *E* none of these

4. Michael and Meg are brother and sister. Meg has three times as many brothers as sisters, but Michael has the same number of brothers as sisters. How many children are there in the family?

   A 4   *B* 5   *C* 6   *D* 7   *E* 8

5. The diagram is a sketch road map of roads linking the two villages of Hear and Thair, passing through Underhill, Kedgeworth, Smallwell, Maun and Churchwake. The number on each section of road is the length (in km) of that road. How long is the shortest route from Hear to Thair?

   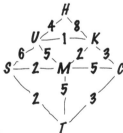

   A 9 km   *B* 10 km   *C* 11 km   *D* 12 km   *E* 13 km

6. One-third of the people at a party are women, a quarter are girls, one-sixth are men and there are six boys. How many people were at the party?

   A 12   *B* 24   *C* 36   *D* 48   *E* can't be sure

7. Mr Bun is baking. His cake recipe specifies 60 g butter, 90 g sugar and 150 g flour. He has enough butter and sugar but only 120 g of flour. How much less sugar and butter must he use to get a correctly balanced mixture?

    A   15 g butter, 22.5 g sugar
    B   15 g butter, 18 g sugar
    C   12 g butter, 22.5 g sugar
    D   12 g butter, 18 g sugar
    E   30 g butter, 30 g sugar

8. My ruler has become worn with age. The only marks left on it are as shown. Which set of distances can I *not* measure directly?

    | 0 1   3   7   12 |

    A 2, 4, 6   B 3, 5, 11   C 3, 7, 9   D 4, 6, 9   E 4, 8, 12

9. All cats are animals, have whiskers and purr. Which statement follows logically from these facts?

    A   any animal which purrs is a cat
    B   some cats don't purr
    C   some cats have whiskers
    D   any animal with whiskers also purrs
    E   an animal with whiskers is always a cat

10. A crossnumber is like a crossword except that the answers are numbers with one digit in each square.

    What is the sum of all the digits in the solution to this crossnumber?

    CLUES
    Across (A)
    1. 2D − 1D
    3. Square of 5D
    4. 3A × 5D
    Down (D)
    1. 2D − 1A
    2. 1D + 1A
    5. 4A ÷ 3A

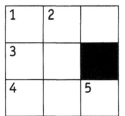

    A 20   B 24   C 30   D 35   E 36

PAPER 16

1. Which number is closest in value to $1992 \div 0.5$?

    A 0 B 990 C 1000 D 2000 E 4000

2. The average age of six children is 13 years and 5 months. A seventh child joins the group, increasing the average age by two months. How old is this seventh child?

    A 13 yr 7 mo B 13 yr 9 mo C 14 yr 5 mo D 14 yr 7 mo E 14 yr 9 mo

3. Four of these give the same answer. Which one is different?

    A $1 - (2 \times 3) + 4$ B $1 + (2 - 3 \times 4) \div 5$ C $((1 \times 2 - 3) - 4) \div 5$
    D $(1 \times 2) - 3$ E $(1 - 2) - 3 \div 4$

4. What is the angle between the hour and minute hands of an ordinary clock showing 7.45?

    A $30°$ B $37.5°$ C $45°$ D $52°$ E $60°$

5. If I drive home with an average speed of 60 mph I will arrive an hour earlier than expected. If I average 40 mph I will arrive an hour later than expected. At what speed should I travel in order to arrive bang on time?

    A 20 mph B 48 mph C 50 mph D 52 mph E 100 mph

6. How many days are there from the vernal equinox (21 March) to the autumnal equinox (23 September) each year?

    A 182 B 183 C 184 D 185 E 186

7. A snooker ball rolls from the point P: $(1, 3)$ straight to X: $(0, 1)$ and then rebounds in the normal way. If it were to go on for ever without slowing down, which of these points would it never pass through?

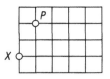

    A $(2, 1)$ B $(2, 2)$ C $(3, 3)$ D $(4, 1)$ E $(5, 3)$

8. In this magic square the numbers in each row, in each column, and in each diagonal have the same sum. What is the value of $U + K + J + M + C$?

    A 20 B 21 C 23 D 24 E 26

9. All except one of these shapes can be cut into two pieces so that the cross-section is an equilateral triangle. Which is the odd one out?

    A a cube B a regular tetrahedron C a square-based pyramid
          D a regular octahedron E a general cuboid

10. The diagram shows a triangle divided up into smaller triangles. If T is the total number of triangles in the figure and P is the total number of parallelograms in the figure, which of the following is true?

    A $T = P$ B $T = 2P$ C $T = P - 2$ D $T = P + 2$ E $T = \dfrac{P}{2}$

PAPER 17

1. What is the largest prime factor of 1992?

    A 2   *B* 3   *C* 83   *D* 249   *E* 1992

2. Four of the angles below are angles in the same quadrilateral. Which is the odd one out?

    A 56°   *B* 74°   *C* 83°   *D* 104°   *E* 117°

3. Which of the following is closest to 19.9×199?

    A 4000   *B* 3990   *C* 3980   *D* 3970   *E* 3960

4. The average of six numbers is 4. A seventh number is added and the new average is 5. What was the seventh number?

    A 1   *B* 5   *C* 6   *D* 11   *E* 12

5. The diagram is a sketch road map of roads linking the villages of Hear, Underhill, Kedgeworth, Smallwell, Maun, Churchwake and Thair. The number on each road is the distance between the two ends. Postman Pat lives in Hear, and has to visit the other six villages before returning home. How long is his shortest route?

    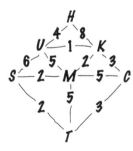

    A 22 km   *B* 23 km   *C* 26 km   *D* 27 km   *E* 28 km

6. Which of these points lies on both of the lines $3x - y = 12$ and $4x + y = 23$?

    A (6, 6)   *B* (4, 7)   *C* (5, 3)   *D* (11, 21)   *E* (5, −3)

7. Little Shera's paddling pool holds 2000 litres of water. It is filled using a hosepipe through which water passes at a rate of 0.04 m^3 per minute. How long does it take to fill the pool?

   A 2 min B 5 min C 8 min D 20 min E longer

8. Most books nowadays have an ISBN or International Standard Book Number. This consists of a nine-digit number followed by a *check digit*. The check digit is calculated by multiplying the first digit by 1, the second by 2, the third by 3, and so on up to the ninth digit (by 9), then adding these nine answers together and finally dividing the total by 11: the *remainder* is then written as the *check digit*. For a particular book the first nine digits are 033343550. What is the check digit?

   A 0 B 4 C 8 D 12 E none of these

9. If $p * q$ means $2p^2 + q$, what does $2 * 5$ mean?

   A 10 B 13 C 21 D 81 E 98

10. The symbol 25! denotes the product of all whole numbers from 1 up to 25. If we calculate its actual value, how many zeros will there be at the end?

   A 1 B 3 C 4 D 5 E 6

PAPER 18

1. The sixth prime number is

    A 6   *B* 9   *C* 11   *D* 13   *E* 17

2. I want to cut a long strip of metal into four shorter pieces. If each cut takes twice as long as the previous one, and the first takes one second, how long will the job take?

    A 3 s   *B* 4 s   *C* 6 s   *D* 7 s   *E* 15 s

3. Which fraction is the smallest?

    A $\frac{9}{14}$ *B* $\frac{8}{13}$ *C* $\frac{14}{19}$ *D* $\frac{15}{28}$ *E* $\frac{7}{15}$

4. The diagram (not drawn accurately) shows a regular pentagon with its centre at O. Calculate the size of the angle x.

    A 36°   *B* 54°   *C* 60°   *D* 72°   *E* 108°

5. *DEFG* is a square which is drawn on the outside of a regular pentagon *ABCDE*. How big is angle *EAF*?

    A 9°   *B* 12°   *C* 15°   *D* 18°   *E* 21°

6. When Gulliver awoke in Lilliput he found the people there were only six inches tall, compared with his own six feet. Everything else in Lilliput was similarly reduced in size. How many Lilliputian 'pint-size' bottles of milk would be needed to provide the human half-pint needed for Gulliver's cornflakes?

    A 6   *B* 36   *C* 72   *D* 216   *E* 864

7. If x and y are positive numbers, which of the following is largest?

   A xy *B* $x^2 + y^2$ *C* $(x+y)^2$ *D* $x^2 + y(y+x)$ *E* can't be sure

8. A sequence of isosceles triangles is constructed starting with $AB = BC$, then $BC = CD$, and so on. If $\angle BAC = 17°$, how many such triangles can be drawn?

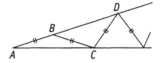

   A 3 only   *B* 4 only   *C* 5 only

        D 6 only   *E* as many as you like

9. A golf competition takes place over 18 holes. At each hole a player gets either a 'bogey', or a 'par', or a 'birdie'. He scores one point for a 'bogey', two points for a 'par', and three points for a 'birdie'. In his round of 18 holes Ian scores twice as many birdies as bogeys, and scores par on all the other holes. If his final score was 39 points, at how many holes did he get a 'par'?

   A 3   *B* 6   *C* 9   *D* 12   *E* 18

10. My house number has the curious property that $\frac{1}{7}$ of it times $\frac{1}{13}$ of it equals the number. What answer should I get when I add the digits of my house number together?

   A 10   *B* 11   *C* 12   *D* 14   *E* 16

PAPER 19

1. The sum of the six marked angles in the diagram is

   A 180°   *B* 270°   *C* 360°   *D* 450°   *E* can't be sure

2. If 2^2 is multiplied by 2^3, what is the answer?

   A 2^5 *B* 2^6 *C* 4^5 *D* 4^6 *E* 4^8

3. Donna has twice as many marbles as Sharon. But if Donna were to give Sharon twenty marbles, Sharon would have three times as many as Donna. How many marbles does Donna have?

   A 20   *B* 24   *C* 28   *D* 30   *E* 32

4. The only prime number in the nineties is

   A 91   *B* 93   *C* 95   *D* 97   *E* 99

5. *Mathematical Pie* is a magazine for pupils at school. The cost per copy depends on how many copies a school orders. In 1988, 1 copy cost 27p; 2 copies cost 21p each; 3–6 copies cost 18p each; 7–39 copies cost 16p each; 40–149 copies cost 15p each.* If your school bought 18 copies of one issue (in 1988), how much change would they have got from £5?

   A £0.14   *B* £1.22   *C* £2.12   *D* £2.88   *E* £4.84

6. What is the square root of 17 956?

   A 124   *B* 126   *C* 127   *D* 134   *E* 136

---

* If you want to order copies, ring 0116 270 3877 to check current prices.

7. In the diagram lengths are marked in cm.
   What is the area of the figure in cm²?

   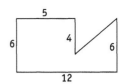

   A 30   *B* 48   *C* 58   *D* 72   *E* 92

8. Matty Matix has bought a lottery ticket numbered 68. Altogether 100 tickets were sold. Which of the following expressions represents the probability that he wins first prize?

   A $\frac{1}{100}$ *B* 0.68   *C* 6.8%   *D* 1 to 100   *E* $\frac{32}{68}$

9. You have to move three discs to make an equilateral triangle the other way up. What is the total of the numbers on the three discs you have to move?

   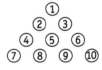

   A 6   *B* 10   *C* 11   *D* 15   *E* 18

10. The time taken for a simple pendulum 1 metre long to swing from side to side and back again is roughly 2 seconds. Which of these is closest to the time taken for a pendulum 2 metres long to swing from side to side and back again?

   A 1 s   *B* 2 s   *C* 3 s   *D* 4 s   *E* 5 s

PAPER 20

1. In a small café the average pay of the five workers is £120 per week. If the four waiters get an average of £100 per week, how much does the cook get ?

    A £80   *B* £125   *C* £140   *D* £180   *E* £200

2. How big is the angle between SSE and WNW?

    A 90°   *B* $112\frac{1}{2}°$ *C* 135°   *D* $157\frac{1}{2}°$ *E* 180°

3. What is the largest prime factor of 1998?

    A 2   *B* 3   *C* 11   *D* 37   *E* 111

4. The median of a list of numbers is the middle number when they are written in numerical order. What is the median of the prime numbers between 8 and 32?

    A 17   *B* 19   *C* 21   *D* 23   *E* 25

5. Which of the four regions is biggest?

    A   *B*   *C*   *D*   *E* two or more are equal biggest

6. What is the remainder when 2^{50} is divided by 10?

    A 2   *B* 4   *C* 6   *D* 8   *E* 0

7. Each of the following equations has either $x = 2$ or $x = 3$ as a solution. Which of them has both $x = 2$ and $x = 3$ as solutions?

    A $3x + 5 = 4x + 2$ *B* $2(2x - 4) = 3(2x - 6)$ *C* $x^2 - 5x + 6 = 0$
    D $(x + 1)^2 = (5 - x)^2$ *E* $\frac{1}{x} + \frac{1}{2x} = \frac{1}{2}$

8. You have to place the numbers 1, 2, 3, 4, 5 in the five squares so that the numbers always decrease from left to right as you go along each row and from top to bottom as you go down each column. One way is shown. How many *other* ways are there of doing this?

5	4	1
3	2	

    A 0   *B* 2   *C* 3   *D* 4   *E* 5

9. One of Baby's birthday presents was a large wooden die in the shape of a cube, which fits snugly in its transparent plastic container. How many different ways are there of fitting the die into its container?

    A 6   *B* 12   *C* 16   *D* 24   *E* 48

10. The following 'proof' that $1 = 2$ contains a mathematical error. In which line (A, B, C, D or E) does this error occur?

            Let $a = b$

    A $\therefore$ $ab = b^2$

    B $\therefore$ $ab - a^2 = b^2 - a^2$

    C $\therefore$ $a(b - a) = (b + a)(b - a)$

    D $\therefore$ $a = b + a$

    E $\therefore$ when $a = 1$ and $b = 1$, we get $1 = 1 + 1 = 2$.

PAPER 21

1. Here are five fractions. Which is the biggest?

   A 62% B $\frac{3}{5}$ C $\frac{2}{3}$ D $1.81 \div 3$ E $\frac{5}{8}$

2. A ladder 2 m long is leaning against a wall. The foot of the ladder is 1 m from the foot of the wall. What is the angle between the ladder and the ground?

   A 30° B 45° C 60° D 75° E 90°

3. In how many different ways can you give exactly 55p change using only 50p, 20p, 10p and 5p coins?

   A 10 B 11 C 12 D 13 E 14

4. Tearaway the tortoise walks at 3 ms^{-1} and runs at 5 ms^{-1}. If she runs for two minutes and then walks for four minutes, what is her average speed?

   A $1\frac{1}{3}$ ms^{-1} B $3\frac{2}{3}$ ms^{-1} C $3\frac{5}{6}$ ms^{-1} D 4 ms^{-1} E $4\frac{1}{3}$ ms^{-1}

5. Two lights mark the entrance to a harbour. One light flashes every seven seconds, the other flashes every six seconds. They both flashed together at 2.00 am. I started observing them exactly five minutes later. How many seconds did I have to wait before I saw them flash together?

   A 6 B 21 C 36 D 37 E 42

6. What is the perimeter of this six-sided figure?

   A 33 B 39 C 48 D 66 E can't be sure

7. 1 January in the year 1995 was on a Sunday. What day must Christmas Day of the same year have been?

    A Monday   *B* Tuesday   *C* Wednesday   *D* Thursday   *E* Saturday

8. London has longitude 0°; Cardiff has the same latitude as London, but has longitude 3° W. On Midsummer's Day the sun rises in London at 4.43 am (BST). At what time does the sun rise that day in Cardiff?

    A 4.31 am   *B* 4.37 am   *C* 4.43 am   *D* 4.49 am   *E* 4.55 am

9. In January Billy Brains opens a garage and starts selling petrol at £1.96 per gallon. In February he discovers that he is losing money fast, so puts up his prices by 25%. By March he finds this has made things worse, so cuts his prices by 20%. By how much do his prices now differ from those in January?

    A −5%   *B* −1%   *C* 0%   *D* +5%   *E* 45%

10. I put vertical mirrors along two sides of a 4 by 4 checkerboard as shown. How many black squares can I see (including the originals) when I look in the mirrors?

    A 8   *B* 16   *C* 24   *D* 32   *E* 40

PAPER 22

1. How many prime numbers less than ten thousand have digits adding up to 2?

    A 1   *B* 2   *C* 3   *D* 4   *E* 5

2. Three youngsters are going to the fair. Each has a whole number of pounds, no-one has more than £20, and the average amount is £16. What is the smallest possible amount one of them could have?

    A £8   *B* £9   *C* £10   *D* £12   *E* £14

3. I am over forty. If I triple my age (in years), then add 29, subtract 11, multiply by two-thirds, add 8, divide by 2 and subtract my age, what will the answer be?

    A 0   *B* 10   *C* 18   *D* 27   *E* can't be sure

4. Two cardboard squares with side lengths 4 cm and 3 cm overlap with one corner of the smaller square at the centre of the larger square. If the overlapping portions are removed, what is the difference between the two remaining areas?

    A 1 cm²   *B* 3 cm²   *C* 5 cm²   *D* 7 cm²   *E* can't be sure

5. Ten points are marked round the circumference of a circle. What is the maximum number of chords that can be drawn joining these points such that no two chords cross each other?

    A 15   *B* 17   *C* 27   *D* 35   *E* 45

6. Jim can type one character per second. How long would it take him to type a list of the numbers from 1 to 100 (inclusive) including a comma between each two successive numbers? (This is how he starts: 1,2,3, ...)

    A 4min 51s   *B* 3min 20s   *C* 4min 48s   *D* 3min 12s   *E* 4min 52s

7. A square is divided into five equal rectangles as shown. Each of these rectangles has perimeter 24 cm. What is the perimeter of the original square?

 A 40 cm   *B* 48 cm   *C* 60 cm   *D* 84 cm   *E* 120 cm

8. A man's stride is 80 cm, his son's is 25 cm. Roughly how many more strides does the boy have to take than his father if they walk together for half a kilometre?

 A 55   *B* 105   *C* 700   *D* 1400   *E* 2000

9. A joke calculator has the labels on the number buttons swopped round. The labels on 0 and 9 have been interchanged, as have the 1 and the 8, the 2 and the 7, and so on. If you enter ⑥ ④ , the calculator thinks you entered 35! Except for this the calculator works normally. Suppose you enter ③ ② ⑦ ⊟ ① ⑥ ⑧ ⊜. What answer will you get?

 A −241   *B* −159   *C* 159   *D* 241   *E* 495

10. What are the least and greatest values for the number of times Friday 13th can occur in any one calendar year?

 A 0 & 2   *B* 0 & 3   *C* 1 & 2   *D* 1 & 3   *E* 1 & 4

PAPER 23

1. Five people share a prize of £17.55. How much does each receive?

    A £3.11   *B* £5.51   *C* £5.11   *D* £3.51   *E* none of these

2. How many of these statements are true?
   (i) 50% of 80 = 80% of 50
   (ii) $\frac{3}{4}$ of 72 = 54
   (iii) $\frac{2}{91} > \frac{2}{93}$
   (iv) $3.106 \div 1.6 > 2$

    A none   *B* one   *C* two   *D* three   *E* all four

3. There are forty-one marbles in a bag, each either red, green, blue or yellow. There are three more red marbles than green marbles, two fewer blue marbles than red marbles, and four more yellow marbles than blue marbles. How many green marbles are there?

    A 8   *B* 9   *C* 10   *D* 11   *E* 13

4. How many small cubes were used to make this block?

    A 1   *B* 9   *C* 10   *D* 13   *E* 14

5. In a class of 24 students, 17 do Latin, 13 do Greek and 8 do Ancient History. What is the smallest possible number of students who take more than one of these subjects?

    A 6   *B* 7   *C* 8   *D* 10   *E* 12

6. Which involves the largest number?

    A   the number of seconds in a year
    B   the length of the Great Wall of China (in cm)
    C   the population of the British Commonwealth
    D   the minutes in an average person's life
    E   the distance from the Earth to the Sun (in km)

7. A clock runs fast, gaining 20 minutes each hour. If the clock is set to the correct time at 8 am, what will the correct time be when the clock next shows 8 o'clock?

    A 4 pm   *B* 5 pm   *C* 12 midnight   *D* 2 am   *E* 12 noon

8. *WXYZ* is a rectangle. *V* is vertically below *T* and *U* is two-thirds of the way up *YZ*. The area of *TUVX* is 12 square units. What is the area of the rectangle *WXYZ*?

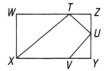

    A 16   *B* 18   *C* 21   *D* 24   *E* 28

9. How many odd numbers between 100 and 1000 remain the same when the digits are written in reverse order?

    A 15   *B* 45   *C* 50   *D* 81   *E* 90

10. What is the angle between the hands of a clock at a quarter to three?

    A 170°   *B* 172.5°   *C* 175°   *D* 177.5°   *E* 180°

PAPER 24

1. The words for the numbers 1 to 10 are listed shortest first, longest last, except that when two words have the same number of letters they are listed in dictionary order. What is the fifth word on the list?

    A one   *B* two   *C* three   *D* four   *E* five

2. I want a set of coins that could be used to make any amount of money from 1p up to 20p. What is the smallest number of coins needed?

    A 2   *B* 4   *C* 5   *D* 6   *E* 7

3. In the diagram $a + b + c + d$ equals

    A 180°   *B* 270°   *C* 360°   *D* 450°   *E* 540°

4. What is the sum of the two missing digits in this multiplication?

    A 6   *B* 8   *C* 10   *D* 12   *E* 14

5. The year 1991 is a palindrome – it reads the same both forwards and backwards. How many other palindromic years have there been altogether since AD1000?

    A 6   *B* 7   *C* 8   *D* 9   *E* 10

6. A mile of pennies, laid in a single line edge to edge, would be worth approximately

    A £50   *B* £100   *C* £200   *D* £400   *E* £800

7. We make 'number chains' starting with a two-figure number by multiplying its digits together; if the answer has two digits, we multiply *them* together; and so on until the answer has only one digit. For example: $86 \rightarrow 48 \rightarrow 32 \rightarrow 6$.
Which of the following starting numbers gives the longest chain?

    A 25   *B* 39   *C* 68   *D* 77   *E* 99

8. The last digit of 2^{1991} is

    A 0   *B* 2   *C* 4   *D* 6   *E* 8

9. In 1991 I went to both France and Germany. When I asked about changing my money, I found that for £1 I could get FFR10.36 (French) or DM3.06 (German). To begin with I got French money only. When I crossed from France into Germany I had about FFR500 left, which I changed into German money. Roughly how much did I get?

    A DM50   *B* DM150   *C* DM300   *D* DM1500   *E* DM5000

10. A crossnumber is like a crossword except that the answers are numbers with one digit in each square.

What is the sum of all eight digits in this crossnumber?

CLUES

Across
1. Square of a prime
4. Prime
5. Square

Down
1. Square of another prime
2. Square
3. Prime

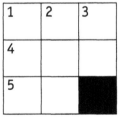

    A 37   *B* 39   *C* 41   *D* 42   *E* 43

PAPER 25

1. How many squares are there altogether in this diagram?

   A 7   *B* 8   *C* 9   *D* 10   *E* 11

2. Arrange the numbers $x = 1375 ÷ 5$, $y = 1656 ÷ 6$, $z = 1897 ÷ 7$ in descending order.

   A xzy   *B* zyx   *C* xyz   *D* yxz   *E* yzx

3. A box containing three bags of potatoes weighs 6.0 kg. When the same box contains five bags of potatoes it weighs 9.2 kg. How heavy is the empty box?

   A 1.2 kg   *B* 1.6 kg   *C* 3.2 kg   *D* 2.0 kg   *E* can't be sure

4. I start out with a square. I then increase one pair of sides by 3 cm and decrease the other pair by 2 cm to form a rectangle. The rectangle has perimeter 26 cm. How long is its longest side?

   A 4 cm   *B* 5 cm   *C* 6 cm   *D* 8 cm   *E* 9 cm

5. Mrs A drives 45 miles from Heathrow to Gatwick round the M25 at an average speed of 63 mph. Mr A leaves Gatwick for Heathrow at the same time as his wife sets out and averages 72 mph. How far are they from Gatwick when they cross?

   A 15 miles   *B* 21 miles   *C* 22.5 miles   *D* 24 miles   *E* 30 miles

6. If six towels on a clothes line take two hours to dry, how long do three similar towels (on the same line) take to dry?

   A 1 hour   *B* 2 hours   *C* 4 hours   *D* 6 hours   *E* 9 hours

7. Which of the following events is the most likely?

    A   an ordinary die will show a six when thrown once

    B   the first card cut from an ordinary pack will be a King or a Queen

    C   three coins tossed simultaneously will all fall showing heads

    D   your first child will be born on a Sunday

    E   a whole number chosen at random will be an exact multiple of 5

8. The ancient Egyptians used this method for finding the area of a circle: take one-ninth of the diameter away from the diameter and square the result. What approximate value of π gives the same answer as the Egyptians' method?

    A $3\frac{1}{7}$ *B* $3\frac{1}{9}$ *C* $3\frac{3}{32}$ *D* $3\frac{13}{81}$ *E* $3\frac{16}{113}$

9. If the equator of a sphere measures 1 m, what is its volume (in m³)?

    A $\frac{1}{6\pi^2}$ *B* $\frac{\pi^3}{6}$ *C* $\frac{1}{\pi}$ *D* $\frac{2}{3}$ *E* π

10. (i) If it rains, you'll get wet.
   (ii) If you get wet, you'll be sorry.
  (iii) If you're not sorry, I'll be cross.
Which of *A*–*E* can be deduced from these facts?

    A   You'll be cross if it rains.

    B   I'll be sorry if you're cross

    C   I'll be sorry if it rains.

    D   You'll be cross if I get wet.

    E   Statements *A*–*D* may all be false.

Paper 26

1. What is the last digit of 19×91?

    A 1   *B* 3   *C* 6   *D* 7   *E* 9

2. Andrea multiplied a number by $1\frac{1}{2}$ and got 18 as an answer. However, she should have divided the number by $1\frac{1}{2}$. What was the correct answer?

    A 8   *B* 12   *C* 18   *D* 27   *E* 36

3. What fraction is halfway between $\frac{1}{3}$ and $\frac{1}{5}$?

    A $\frac{4}{15}$ *B* $\frac{7}{15}$ *C* $\frac{1}{4}$ *D* $\frac{8}{15}$ *E* $\frac{1}{2}$

4. Given that the area of the square is one unit, estimate the area of the other shape.

    A 1   *B* 3   *C* 5   *D* 7   *E* 9

5. Tim's mother says that he is worth his weight in gold. If gold is valued at £300 per ounce, how much does Tim's mother think he is worth?

    A £500 000   *B* £5 000 000   *C* £50 000 000
             D £500 000 000   *E* £5 000 000 000

6. You roll two ordinary dice. What is the probability that neither face shows a prime number?

    A $\frac{1}{9}$ *B* $\frac{1}{4}$ *C* $\frac{4}{9}$ *D* $\frac{9}{16}$ *E* $\frac{3}{4}$

7. 720 720 is divisible without remainder by 1, by 2, by 3, and so on all the way up to where? (Notice that though 720 720 is divisible by 20 it is not divisible by 19, so it is not divisible *all the way up to* 20; nor is it divisible all the way up to 19.)

    A 10   *B* 11   *C* 13   *D* 16   *E* 18

8. Which is the largest of these measurements?

   A 1 fathom   *B* 2 metres   *C* 3 yards   *D* 4 cubits   *E* 5 feet

9. A milkman delivers a total of 336 pints of milk each week to eight houses in a street. Each house has a fixed daily order, but their daily orders are all different. What is the maximum possible number of pints delivered to any one house each day?

   A 6   *B* 14   *C* 20   *D* 42   *E* 48

10. A memorial column 60 m high is built as a cylinder and has a spiral staircase round the outside exactly as shown. If the circumference of the cylinder is 5 m then the length of the staircase is

   A 52 m   *B* 65 m   *C* $\frac{300}{\pi}$ m   *D* $\frac{375}{\pi}$ m   *E* 192 m

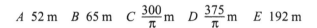

PAPER 27

1. Emma has seven coins: two 1p coins, one 2p, one 5p, one 10p, one 20p and one 50p coin. What is the smallest amount she cannot make using these coins?

    A 13p   *B* 29p   *C* 40p   *D* 41p   *E* 45p

2. 5% of 25% of 4000 equals

    A 32   *B* 50   *C* 125   *D* 200   *E* 500

3. 1991 is divisible by 11 and 1992 is divisible by 12. When will we have a year that is divisible by both 11 and 12?

    A 2003   *B* 2112   *C* 2123   *D* 2124   *E* 2135

4. The angle x is

    A 24°   *B* 33°   *C* 42°   *D* 48°   *E* 66°

5. Rip Van Winkle awoke from his 20-year sleep with no idea where he was or what day it was. He approached a nearby woodsman and asked: 'What day is it?' The woodsman was naturally suspicious at the sight of this curious character with a very long beard, so he answered (truthfully): 'When the day after tomorrow is yesterday, today will be as far from Tuesday as today was from Tuesday when the day before yesterday was tomorrow.' What day was it?

    A Sunday   *B* Monday   *C* Tuesday   *D* Wednesday   *E* Friday

6. Which is the smallest fraction?

    A $\frac{9}{12}$ *B* $\frac{6}{10}$ *C* $\frac{14}{20}$ *D* $\frac{15}{28}$ *E* $\frac{7}{15}$

7. What is the perimeter of this figure?

    A 17   *B* 34   *C* 48   *D* 51   *E* can't be sure

8. Phileas Fogg went round the world (radius 6400 km) in 80 days. What was his approximate average speed (in km/day)?

    A 0   *B* 80   *C* 500   *D* 2000   *E* 500 000

9. The hexagon *ABCDEF* with *AF* = *BC* and *AB* parallel to *FC* just fits inside a circle. *BX* is drawn parallel to *AF*. If ∠*XBC* = 100°, how big is ∠*ABX*?

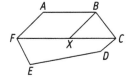

    A 20°   *B* 30°   *C* 35°   *D* 40°   *E* 60°

10. In this division each letter stands for one of the digits 0–9. Different letters stand for different digits. What is the value of *S* + *M* + *C*?

    A 12   *B* 15   *C* 16
              D 18   *E* more than one possible answer

PAPER 28

1. In ancient Egyptian numerals, ⌐ represented one, ∩ represented ten, and ⊙ represented a hundred. What would an ancient Egyptian have understood ⊙⊙⊙⌐⌐ to mean?

   A 23   *B* 32   *C* 203   *D* 302   *E* 99 911

2. *ABCD* is a rectangle. How big is angle *DBE*?

   A 12°   *B* 18°   *C* 42°   *D* 48°   *E* 60°

   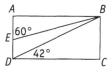

3. The eighth prime number is

   A 11   *B* 13   *C* 17   *D* 19   *E* 23

4. How many letters are there in the correct answer for this question?

   A one   *B* two   *C* three   *D* four   *E* five

5. How many tickets each measuring 60 mm by 40 mm can be cut from a sheet of card measuring 66 cm by 30 cm?

   A none   *B* 77   *C* 81   *D* 82   *E* 82.5

6. A class measured the heights of 1000 men chosen at random. They then drew a histogram to show their results. Which of the following is most like the histogram they drew?

7. When Gill was three years old she enjoyed helping to look after our two guinea pigs Pythagoras and Euclid. Twice each day she fed them one carrot and four lettuce leaves each. An average lettuce leaf contains $1\frac{1}{2}$ calories and an average carrot 5 calories. In making one hop a guinea pig uses 2 calories; each skip uses 3 calories; and each jump uses 7 calories. Guinea pigs hop more than they skip, skip more than they jump, and make at least one hop, one skip and one jump each day. What is the total number of leaps (hops, skips and jumps) each guinea pig could afford to make each day?

     A 6   *B* 7   *C* 8   *D* 9   *E* 10

8. What would be the units digit in the answer to $7353 \times 8209 \times 15879$?

     A 1   *B* 3   *C* 5   *D* 7   *E* 9

9. You want the black and white counters to swap places in as few moves as possible. A move consists of moving a counter one square up, down, to the left or to the right onto an empty square. What is the fewest number of moves required?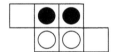

     A 8   *B* 10   *C* 12   *D* 14   *E* 16

10. *PQRSTU* is a regular hexagon of area 1 cm². *V* is the reflection of *R* in *QS*. What is the area of the hexagon *PQVSTU* (in cm²)?

     A $\frac{1}{2}$ *B* $\frac{3}{5}$ *C* $\frac{2}{3}$ *D* $\frac{3}{4}$ *E* $\frac{5}{6}$

PAPER 29

1. The smallest number which is divisible by 2, by 3, by 4, by 5 and by 6 is

    A 12   *B* 30   *C* 60   *D* 120   *E* 720

2. The L-shape shown here is cut into isosceles right-angled triangles. What is the smallest possible number of pieces?

    A 2   *B* 3   *C* 4   *D* 5   *E* 6

3. 324 is divided in the ratio 1:2. The smaller part is then divided in the ratio 3:1. How big is the smallest of the three parts?

    A 27   *B* 54   *C* 81   *D* 108   *E* 216

4. A train 100 m long is travelling at a speed of 90 km per hour when it comes to a tunnel 300 m long. How long will it take for the train to pass completely through the tunnel?

    A 4 s   *B* 8 s   *C* 12 s   *D* 16 s   *E* 20 s

5. The Pharaoh Chaot IX planned a grand pyramid 100 m high to be buried in. The builder ran out of stone when it was only 75 m high and left it with a flat top. He was buried alive! If he had been paid *pro rata*, what fraction of the agreed price would he have received?

    A $\frac{27}{64}$ *B* $\frac{9}{16}$ *C* $\frac{3}{4}$ *D* $\frac{15}{16}$ *E* $\frac{63}{64}$

6. Which number is closest to the square root of 200 000 000?

    A 1400   *B* 4500   *C* 14 000   *D* 45 000   *E* 100 000 000

7. The volume (in cubic units) of the solid shown here is

    A 51   *B* 120   *C* 60   *D* 24   *E* 45

8. Each letter stands for one of the digits 1–9. Different letters stand for different digits. If *W* stands for 3, what is *H*?

    A 1   *B* 4   *C* 6   *D* 8   *E* 9

9. A fly starts out at the corner marked *X* on the cube shown here and sets out along the edge *XA*. Each time she reaches a corner she turns left (*L*) or right (*R*). If the sequence of turns she makes goes *LRLLRRLLLRRR*, at which corner does she finish?

    A   *B*   *C*   *D*   *E*

10. What is the perimeter of this figure?

    A 12   *B* 28   *C* 32   *D* 192   *E* can't be sure

PAPER 30

1. What sort of triangle has two sides of length 10 cm and 5 cm and an angle of 60° between these two sides?

    A equilateral   *B* isosceles   *C* scalene
          D right-angled   *E* can't be sure

2. Mum gave me £10 for my birthday and told me to take myself and some friends to the cinema. It cost £1.75 to get in. How many friends could I take with me?

    A 4   *B* 5   *C* 6   *D* 8   *E* 11

3. Express the fraction $\frac{216}{243}$ in its lowest terms.

    A $\frac{216}{243}$ *B* $\frac{72}{81}$ *C* $\frac{24}{27}$ *D* $\frac{16}{43}$ *E* $\frac{8}{9}$

4. My class of Martian 14-year-olds consists of ungi pupils. Each Martian has arfungi legs. How many legs are there in the class I teach?

    A ungi × (1 + arfungi)   *B* arf   *C* ungi + arfungi
          D ungi × arfungi + 2   *E* (ungi + 1) × arfungi

5. A square has three of its corners at (1, 3), (4, 0), (4, 6). Where is the fourth corner?

    A (7, 3)   *B* (2, 5)   *C* (5, 2)   *D* (3, 7)   *E* (3, 5)

6. In addition to spanning a river 60 m wide, a bridge overlaps each bank. One-third of the bridge overlaps one bank and one-half overlaps the other bank. What is the total length of the bridge in metres?

    A 300   *B* 180   *C* 360   *D* 120   *E* 110

7. The long edges of a ruler are usually marked in opposite directions so that the scale on the top edge always runs from left to right. My 19 cm ruler has one side marked in cm, the other in mm. What is opposite the 10 mm mark?

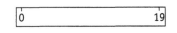

    A 1 cm   *B* 9 cm   *C* 10 cm   *D* 18 cm   *E* 90 mm

8. How many factors (including 1 and 1990) has 1990?

    A 2   *B* 3   *C* 4   *D* 6   *E* 8

9. In the diagram $AB = 6$ cm, $AC = 10$ cm, $DE = 4$ cm. What is the length of AD (in cm)?

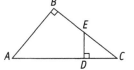

    A $4\frac{2}{3}$ *B* $5\frac{1}{3}$ *C* $7\frac{1}{2}$ *D* $6\frac{2}{3}$ *E* 8

10. The only buttons that work on my calculator are 4, +, −, ×, ÷ and =. To get 2 on the screen I could press 4 + 4 = ÷ 4 =, a total of seven button presses. Which of the following numbers takes the fewest button presses?

    A 7   *B* 9   *C* 10   *D* 11   *E* 20

PAPER 31

1. What is the units digit of the answer to $23 \times 79 \times 58$?

    A 0 $\qquad$ B 2 $\qquad$ C 4 $\qquad$ D 5 $\qquad$ E 6

2. How many different ways are there of paying exactly 10p?

    A 7 $\qquad$ B 8 $\qquad$ C 9 $\qquad$ D 10 $\qquad$ E 11

3. In an isosceles triangle one angle is twice as big as another. How big is the smallest angle in the triangle?

    A 30° $\qquad$ B 36° $\qquad$ C 45° $\qquad$ D 60° $\qquad$ E can't be sure

4. My car averages 27 miles per gallon on a long journey. How many gallons should be just enough for a 600 mile journey?

    A 10 $\qquad$ B 20 $\qquad$ C 22 $\qquad$ D 23 $\qquad$ E 30

5. Here are some facts about Fay's exam script.
    (i)   No solution to a geometrical problem was marked wrong.
    (ii) No tidy solution was written in green ink.
    (iii) No erroneous solution scored any marks.
    (iv) All Fay's solutions were written in green ink.
    (v)   No untidy solution was free of errors.
    Which of A–E does *not* follow logically from these facts?

    A Fay scored either zero or full marks on each question
    B Fay answered no geometry questions
    C Fay could not possibly have scored a lower mark
    D Fay got at least one question right
    E Every solution was untidy

6. Two numbers have sum 30 and product 144. What is their difference?

    A 0 $\qquad$ B 2 $\qquad$ C 12 $\qquad$ D 18 $\qquad$ E 114

7. 1988 in Roman numerals is

    A MCMLXXXVIII   *B* MCMXXCIIX   *C* MDCCCCLXXXVIII
       D MDCDXXCIIX   *E* XIIMM

8. The table on the right shows the result of multiplying any two of *A*, *B*, *C*, *D* and *E*. For example, *D* ∗ *B* = *A*. What is *A* ∗ *B* ∗ *C* ∗ *D* ∗ *E* equal to?

∗	A	B	C	D	E
A	B	C	D	E	A
B	C	D	E	A	B
C	D	E	A	B	C
D	E	A	B	C	D
E	A	B	C	D	E

    A   *B*   *C*   *D*   *E*

9. Each letter stands for one of the digits 0–9. Different letters stand for different digits. How many different solutions are there?

    A none   *B* one   *C* two   *D* three   *E* four

10. Which net can be folded to make a piece which combines with the base shown on the right to form a cube?

    A   *B*   *C*

      D   *E*

PAPER 32

1. According to British Rail measurements along the track, Durham is $269\frac{1}{4}$ miles south of Aberdeen and London is 524 miles from Aberdeen. How far is Durham from London (in miles)?

    A $254\frac{1}{4}$ B $254\frac{3}{4}$ C $255\frac{1}{4}$ D $255\frac{3}{4}$ E $793\frac{1}{4}$

2. Which of the following four-sided shapes can never have two different-sized angles?

    A kite B parallelogram C rectangle
              D rhombus E trapezium

3. Which one of these numbers is the average of the other four?

    A 25 B 11 C 21 D 20 E 23

4. The perimeter of a triangle is 24 cm. Its sides have lengths (in cm) which are consecutive numbers. How long is its shortest side?

    A 6 cm B 7 cm C 8 cm D 9 cm E 10 cm

5. Which of the following is *not* the net of a triangular prism?

    A B C

    D E

6. Gill has given up trying to spell and uses her blocks to build towers. Each block is a cube of side 6 cm and she is trying to make the tower lean over as far as possible without tipping over. The top block overlaps the one below it by half its side, which overhangs by $\frac{1}{4}$ of its side the one below that, which overhangs by $\frac{1}{6}$ of its side the one below that, which overhangs the bottom block by $\frac{1}{8}$ of its side. What is the total overhang (in cm)?

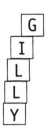

    A $1\frac{1}{5}$ *B* $5\frac{1}{2}$ *C* $6\frac{1}{4}$ *D* $12\frac{1}{4}$ *E* 24

7. A set of dominoes contains every possible combination of two numbers between 0 and 6 inclusive, including two numbers the same. How many spots are there altogether on a set of dominoes?

    A 84   *B* 105   *C* 126   *D* 147   *E* 168

8. *ABCDEFGH* is a regular octagon. Which triangle has the largest area?

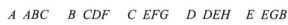

    A ABC   *B CDF*   *C EFG*   *D DEH*   *E EGB*

9. Each of the numbers 74, 83, 92 has digits adding to a multiple of 11. How big is the gap between 92 and the *next but one* such number?

    A 9   *B* 18   *C* 27   *D* 36   *E* 45

10. What is the area of the octagon inside this 6 cm by 6 cm square?

    A 20 cm² *B* 24 cm² *C* 28 cm² *D* 30 cm² *E* 32 cm²

PAPER 33

1. You are allowed to use only the digits 1, 2 and 3 but you may use each digit as often as you like. How many different three-digit numbers is it possible to make?

    A 6   *B* 12   *C* 24   *D* 27   *E* 30

2. When the following decimals are arranged in order of size, which one will be in the middle?

    A 0.16   *B* 0.61   *C* 0.016   *D* 0.061   *E* 0.106

3. There are 4.54 litres in a gallon. Roughly how many gallons are there in 100 litres?

    A 454   *B* 104.54   *C* 25   *D* 22   *E* 20

4. If a hen and a half lays an egg and a half in a day and a half, how long does it take a hen to lay one egg (in days)?

    A $\frac{2}{3}$ *B* 1   *C* $1\frac{1}{2}$ *D* 2   *E* 3

5. Using exactly 24 identical small cubes you can make a cuboid. How many different cuboids can you make using all 24 identical small cubes each time?

    A 2   *B* 3   *C* 4   *D* 5   *E* 6

6. Little Bo Peep has promised not to lose any more sheep. She starts to make a sheep pen *PQRS* using an existing wall for the side *PS* and three hurdles of lengths 2 m, 3 m and 5 m (in some order) for the sides *PQ*, *QR*, *RS*. If the angles at *Q* and *R* are at right angles, what is the largest area Bo Peep can get?

    A 8 m²   *B* 10 m²   *C* $10\frac{1}{2}$ m²   *D* $12\frac{1}{2}$ m²   *E* can't be sure

7. A normal family car is travelling at 60 mph. Roughly how many times does each wheel rotate each second?

   A 4   *B* 14   *C* 40   *D* 60   *E* 100

8. The probability that it rains while Susan is walking home from school is $\frac{1}{3}$; the probability that Susan remembers to take her umbrella is $\frac{3}{5}$. If these events are independent, what is the probability Susan gets wet walking home?

   A $\frac{1}{5}$ *B* $\frac{2}{5}$ *C* $\frac{2}{15}$ *D* $\frac{11}{15}$ *E* $\frac{14}{15}$

9. If you are allowed to use positive whole numbers and addition, there are just four different ways of writing the number 3, namely: 1+1+1, 2+1, 1+2 and 3 itself. How many ways are there of writing the number 5?

   A 7   *B* 9   *C* 10   *D* 14   *E* 16

10. How many axes of rotational symmetry has a cube?

   A 3   *B* 4   *C* 7   *D* 12   *E* 13

1. Which is the smallest prime number among the following?

   A 147   B 157   C 167   D 177   E 187

2. A piece of paper is cut out and labelled as shown in the
   diagram. It is folded along the dotted lines to make an open
   box. If the box is placed on a table so that the top of the box
   is open, then the label on the bottom of the box is

   A   B   C   D   E

3. $\frac{1}{5}$ is called the *reciprocal* of 5. The sum of the reciprocals of all the factors of 24 is

   A $2\frac{11}{24}$ B $2\frac{1}{2}$ C $2\frac{5}{24}$ D $1\frac{11}{24}$ E $1\frac{1}{2}$

4. If X is a multiple of 8, and Y is a multiple of 12, what is the largest number which
   $X + Y$ is necessarily a multiple of?

   A 1   B 2   C 4   D 20   E 24

5. If I dial 42904 on this push-button telephone, which of the
   following shapes does my finger *not* trace out?

   A parallelogram   B polygon   C quadrilateral
            D rectangle   E trapezium

6. Some people believe that their fortunes are controlled by biorhythms. There are three of these rhythms: the physical rhythm has a high point every 23 days, the mental rhythm every 33 days, and the emotional rhythm every 28 days. Today Michelle feels lucky: she is at a high point in all three rhythms at once. How long will it be before that happens again?

   A 28 days   *B* 84 days   *C* about 1 year
        D about 6 years   *E* about 58 years

7. The first diagram has three spikes, the second has six spikes. How many spikes would you expect on the fourth diagram?

   A 24   *B* 36   *C* 54   *D* 66   *E* 72

8. In the quadrilateral shown here, with the lengths and angles given, what is the length of *PS*?

   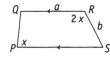

   A b *B* $a + b$ *C* $a + 2b$ *D* $2a + b$ *E* can't be sure

9. Roughly how many adults weigh the same as an average car?

   A 4   *B* 10   *C* 50   *D* 100   *E* 200

10. A set of traffic lights runs through the following sequence: red (90 s), red and amber (5 s), green (80 s), amber (5 s), then back to red, and so on. For how many minutes is the red light on during the course of 24 hours?

    A 720   *B* 760   *C* 2160   *D* 43 200   *E* 45 600

PAPER 35

1. Use the digits 1, 2, 3, 4 once each to form two two-digit numbers with the largest possible product. What is this product?

    A 322   *B* 903   *C* 1302   *D* 1312   *E* 1376

2. One whole brick weighs 5 kg and half a brick. How much does one brick weigh?

    A $3\frac{1}{3}$ kg   *B* 5 kg   *C* $7\frac{1}{2}$ kg   *D* $8\frac{1}{3}$ kg   *E* 10 kg

3. A rope fifty metres long is cut into two pieces. One piece is three-sevenths the length of the other. How long is the shorter piece (in metres)?

    A 15   *B* 20   *C* $21\frac{3}{7}$ *D* $28\frac{4}{7}$ *E* 35

4. My age added to three more than my age gives four times my daughter's age minus five. The sum of our ages is fifty-nine. How old is my daughter?

    A 13   *B* 14   *C* 15   *D* 21   *E* can't be sure

5. How many tickets, each 8 cm by 6 cm, can I cut from a sheet of card 30 cm by 21 cm, if I use the card as efficiently as possible?

    A 9   *B* 10   *C* 11   *D* 12   *E* 13

6. Reasonable quality writing paper is often 100 gsm: that is, a piece of paper with area one square metre would weigh 100 g. What is the approximate weight of one A4 sheet of 100 gsm quality paper?

    A 2 g   *B* 4 g   *C* 6 g   *D* 8 g   *E* 10 g

7. How many different cardboard triangles can be cut out, each with sides of length a whole number of centimetres, and each with perimeter 15 cm?

    A 3   *B* 5   *C* 7   *D* 12   *E* 19

8. An equilateral triangle and a regular hexagon have equal perimeters. What is the ratio of their areas?

   A 1:4   *B* 2:3   *C* 1:1   *D* 3:2   *E* 2:1

9. A coin is tossed 100 times and lands heads 60 times and tails 40 times. If it is tossed once more, which of these is true?

   A it will definitely land 'heads'
   B it will definitely land 'tails'
   C it is more likely to land 'tails' than 'heads'
   D it is more likely to land 'heads' than 'tails'
   E the chances of 'heads' and 'tails' are equal

10. An *abundant* number is one whose factors (not including the number itself) add up to more than the number itself. For example, the factors of 8 are 1, 2 and 4 and $1 + 2 + 4$ is *less than* 8, so 8 is *not* abundant. How many abundant numbers are there below 30?

    A 1   *B* 2   *C* 3   *D* 4   *E* 5

PAPER 36

1. 9 has three factors only (1, 3 and 9). Which of these numbers has three factors only?

   A 81   *B* 121   *C* 225   *D* 441   *E* 625

2. The angles of a triangle are all perfect squares. What is the size of the smallest angle?

   A 9°   *B* 16°   *C* 25°   *D* 36°   *E* can't be sure

3. One of these numbers cannot be factorised as the product of three prime numbers. Which one is it?

   A 30   *B* 42   *C* 70   *D* 90   *E* 182

4. If we add the digits of 1992 we get $1 + 9 + 9 + 2 = 21$; if we then add the digits of 21 we get a single digit $2 + 1 = 3$, so we say that 1992 has *digital sum* 3. Which of these years also has digital sum 3?

   A 1921   *B* 1932   *C* 1958   *D* 1974   *E* 2002

5. A fraction $\frac{x}{y}$ is such that when I add 8 to x and 12 to y the value of the fraction is unchanged. What could the pair x, y be?

   A 1, 3   *B* 5, 10   *C* 9, 12   *D* 10, 15   *E* 12, 16

6. The diagram illustrates the paths down a mountainside from the top *T* to the bottom *B*. Shona starts at the top and walks downwards to *B*. Whenever the path divides, she makes a choice. How many different routes can she take from *T* to *B*?

   A 2   *B* 4   *C* 5   *D* 8   *E* 9

7. The letters in this 'letter-sum' stand for digits. Different letters stand for different digits. What must T stand for?

$$\begin{array}{r} T H I S \\ I S + \\ \hline H A R D \end{array}$$

    A 1 B 5 C 6 D 7 E 8

8. Vincent Van Gogh's painting 'Irises' fetched £31 million recently, which works out at about £30 000 for an area the size of a postage stamp. A Mauritius 'Penny Red' stamp was expected to fetch £1 million in a more recent sale. If 'Penny Reds' were stuck all over the Van Gogh canvas, roughly how much would the stamps be worth?

    A £1000 B £33m C £970m D £1030m E £31 billion

9. You have to insert three of the four operations $+, -, \times, \div$ in the gaps of this sum to make the equation correct. (There may be more than one way of doing this.) Which operation can never be used?

    $$1 = ((2 \ldots 3) \ldots 4) \ldots 5$$

    A + B − C × D ÷ E can't be done

10. Moses is twice as old as Methuselah was when Methuselah was one-third as old as Moses will be when Moses is as old as Methuselah is now. If the difference in their ages is 666, how old is Methuselah?

    A 222 B 666 C 999 D 1332 E 1998

PAPER 37

1. Which of the following cannot possibly be a perfect square?

   A 508 369 B 630 436 C 741 321 D 799 238 E 855 625

2. At different times and in different places different cultures have used different values for π. Which of the following is closest to the true value?

   A 3.1605 (Egypt, $c.$ 2000 BC)
   B 3.14163 (Greece, $c.$ 230 BC)
   C 3.1555 (China, $c.$ AD 250)
   D 3.16 (India, c. AD 550)
   E 3.141818 (Italy, $c.$ AD 1220)

3. Joseph is four years older than twice his sister's age. In four years' time he will be eleven years older than her. How old is Joseph now?

   A 7 B 10 C 16 D 18 E 22

4. What is the largest possible number of 60° angles in a polygon with seven sides?

   A 2 B 3 C 4 D 5 E 7

5. Two consecutive odd numbers have product equal to 899. What is their sum?

   A 60 B 62 C 64 D 66 E can't be sure

6. This is how a game of Noughts and Crosses began. It is X's turn. Where should X go to be absolutely certain of winning on her next go?

   A B C D E

   $$\begin{array}{c|c|c} X & O & X \\ \hline A & B & C \\ \hline D & E & O \end{array}$$

7. Four of the options represent the same fraction. Which is the other one?

   A 0.125 B $\frac{1}{12}+\frac{1}{24}$ C $\frac{1}{8}$ D $12\frac{1}{2}\%$ E $\frac{12}{10}+\frac{5}{100}$

8. The diagram shows two equilateral triangles and a circle which touches the sides of the larger triangle and passes through the vertices of the smaller triangle. What is the ratio of the areas of the two triangles?

    A 1:2   *B* 1:3   *C* 1:4   *D* 1:2√3   *E* 1:3√2

9. P and V are connected by the relation $PV^2 = 4$. If V is doubled, by what is P multiplied?

    A 2   *B* 4   *C* 16   *D* $\frac{1}{16}$ *E* $\frac{1}{4}$

10. The diagram shows a push-button telephone. When dialling 123 6547 with a pencil, the pencil point moves six equal steps. To dial 123 6548 the pencil point has to move slightly further. For which of the following numbers does the pencil point have to move the furthest?

    A 168 5412   *B* 832 5478   *C* 953 6580   *D* 908 5247   *E* 708 9653

PAPER 38

1. The total number of triangles in this picture is

    A 6   *B* 8   *C* 9   *D* 11   *E* 12

2. How many litres of water must be added to 40 litres of a 40% solution to reduce the concentration to 30%?

    A $13\frac{2}{3}$ *B* $12\frac{2}{3}$ *C* 13   *D* $13\frac{1}{3}$ *E* $13\frac{3}{4}$

3. One millionth of a second is called a microsecond. Roughly how long is a microcentury?

    A 1 second   *B* 1 minute   *C* 1 hour   *D* 1 day   *E* 1 week

4. Given that ♠ = ◇ ◇ ◇ and Γ = ♠ ♠, I can write Γ Γ Γ ♠ as a string of ◇ s. How many ◇ s will I need?

    A 6   *B* 8   *C* 9   *D* 18   *E* 21

5. 31 books are arranged from left to right in order of increasing price. Each book costs £2 more or less than its neighbours. The most expensive book costs the same as the middle book and one of its neighbours together. Which of these statements is true?

    A The most expensive book costs £64.
    B The cheapest book costs £4.
    C The middle book costs £36.
    D The two most expensive books would cost £120.
    E The three middle books would cost £96.

6. If twelve typists type twelve thousand twelve hundred and twelve lines in twelve minutes, how many lines would you expect ten typists to type in ten minutes?

    A 9175   *B* 11 010   *C* 13 212   *D* 110 100   *E* 101 010

7. 122 472 is an unusual number. To see why, add its digits together: what do you get? Divide this number into your starting number to get a new number. Now add up the digits of this new number: what do you get? Next divide this into your new number to get an even smaller number. Repeat the process with this smaller number. Carry on until you get a single-figure number. How many divisions must you do *altogether* before ending either with a 1 or with a number which leaves a remainder?

    A 1   *B* 2   *C* 3   *D* 4   *E* 5

8. If your maths teacher were to talk without stopping for a whole hour (what a terrible thought!) roughly how many words would he or she utter?

    A 1000   *B* 3000   *C* 10 000   *D* 30 000   *E* 100 000

9. 'What's the time? Half past nine!' In fact, since 12 o'clock the hands have gone round twice as fast as they should have for half the time, and half as fast as they should have for the other half. What time should the clock show?

    A 3.48   *B* 4.45   *C* 7.00   *D* 7.36   *E* 9.30

10. A pyramid with square base *ABCD* and apex *E* has four equilateral triangular faces. How big is angle *AEC*?

    A ≤60°   *B* between 60° and 90°   *C* exactly 90°
            D between 90° and 120°   *E* ≥120°

PAPER 39

1. £300 is divided in the ratio 2:3. The larger part is then divided into two parts in the ratio 3:2. How big is the smallest of the three parts?

    A £48   *B* £72   *C* £108   *D* £120   *E* £200

2. A circle of radius 10 cm has its radius decreased by 3 cm. By what percentage has its area decreased?

    A 90%   *B* 70%   *C* 51%   *D* 49%   *E* 30%

3. The year 1991 is a palindrome – it reads the same both forwards and backwards. It is also exactly divisible by 11. How many years after 1991 is the next palindromic year which is exactly divisible by 11?

    A 11   *B* 121   *C* 231   *D* 341   *E* 1991

4. Saturn is nearly fifteen hundred million km from the Sun. It revolves around the Sun roughly once every thirty Earth years. What is its approximate average speed (in km per hour)?

    A 1500   *B* 13 000   *C* 25 000   *D* 36 000   *E* 150 000

5. What is the units digit of 19^{90}?

    A 0   *B* 1   *C* 3   *D* 7   *E* 9

6. How many right angles are there in this diagram?

    A 4   *B* 16   *C* 25   *D* 40   *E* 64

7. What is the angle between the hands of a clock at 1.25?

    A 100°   *B* 107.5°   *C* 110°   *D* 120°   *E* 150°

8. A regular hexagon just fits inside a circle of diameter 4 cm. What is the perimeter of the hexagon?

   A 4 cm   *B* 12 cm   *C* 4π cm   *D* 8π cm   *E* hard to say

9. How many different factors does the number 1 002 001 have?

   A 2   *B* 3   *C* 8   *D* 27   *E* at least 30

10. The square has sides of length 20 units. The corners and midpoints of the sides are joined as shown. What is the area (in square units) of the central quadrilateral?

   A 75   *B* 80   *C* 90   *D* 96   *E* 100

PAPER 40

1. You have to use the digits 9, 7, 6, 4, 2, 0 once each to make the smallest possible even six-digit number. Which digit should you put in the hundreds column?

    A 2   *B* 4   *C* 6   *D* 7   *E* 9

2. What fraction has decimal 0.0125?

    A $\frac{1}{125}$ *B* $\frac{1}{8}$ *C* $\frac{1}{80}$ *D* $\frac{11}{4}$ *E* none of these

3. $\angle ABC$ equals

    A 135°   *B* 45°   *C* 60°   *D* 90°   *E* can't be sure

4. A motorist drove from Bristol to Bath at an average speed of 40 mph, and then from Bath to Chippenham at an average speed of 30 mph. What was her average speed for the whole journey?

    A 34 mph   *B* 35 mph   *C* 36 mph
              D 70 mph   *E* need more information

5. Which of these is the largest?

    A 1990   *B* 19 × 90   *C* 1^{990} *D* 19^{90} *E* 199^{0}

6. The diagram (not drawn to scale) shows a circle centre *C*, and *ABCD* is a rectangle. The length *CD* = 6 cm, and *DE* = 3cm. The length *BD* is

    A 8.5 cm   *B* 9 cm   *C* 9.6 cm
              D 10 cm   *E* impossible to find without further information

7. A *perfect* number is a number whose factors (not including itself) add up to that number. For example, the factors of 6 are 1, 2, 3 and 6, and $1 + 2 + 3 = 6$. There is one perfect number between 20 and 30. What is it?

    A 21   *B* 24   *C* 25   *D* 27   *E* 28

8. An octahedron is a solid shape with eight triangular faces, four of which meet at each corner. How many edges does it have?

    A 3   *B* 8   *C* 12   *D* 20   *E* 24

9. The nearest star (other than the Sun) is about four light years away from Earth. If light travels at 300 000 km per second, how far can it travel in four years?

    A 1×10^{11} km   *B* 6×10^{11} km   *C* 2×10^{12} km
        D 9×10^{12} km   *E* 4×10^{13} km

10. There is a unique number formed by the digits 1, 2, 3, 4, 5, 6, 7, 8, 9 which is such that the number formed by the first n digits is divisible by n for all values of n from 1 to 9. This number is

    A 123 456 789   *B* 123 654 897   *C* 963 258 147
        D 381 654 729   *E* 528 416 397

PAPER 41

1. $1 - 2 + 3 - 4 + 5 - 6 + \ldots + 97 - 98 + 99$ equals

       A 0   *B* −50   *C* 49   *D* 48   *E* 50

2. How big is the angle x?

   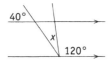

       A 20°   *B* 40°   *C* 60°   *D* 70°   *E* 80°

3. A block of chocolate is divided between three children. Andrea gets two-fifths of the block, Basil gets one-fourth and Cathy has the remaining 28 g. How many grams (to the nearest whole number) does Andrea get?

       A 11   *B* 20   *C* 28   *D* 32   *E* 80

4. Which is shortest?

       A   1994 months
       B   one-sixth of a millenium
       C   two centuries
       D   a million hours
       E   the length of time since the French Revolution

5. Helen cycles steadily for 36 miles. If she had managed to go 3 mph faster she would have taken one hour less. What was her average speed (in mph)?

       A 6   *B* 9   *C* 12   *D* 18   *E* 24

6. The yearly change in the yield of one particular crop in our area over the past four years was 25% increase, then 25% decrease, then 25% decrease and finally a 25% increase. What was the total percentage change in yield over the four years (to the nearest 1%)?

       A −12   *B* −1   *C* 0   *D* 1   *E* 12

7. A windmill has sails whose tips describe a circle of diameter thirty-eight metres. If the centre of the circle is forty metres above the ground, how close to the ground do the tips pass?

   A 1 m   *B* 2 m   *C* 18 m   *D* 21 m   *E* 78 m

8. Which of the following pairs x, y will *not* satisfy the equation $29x - 18y = 15$?

   A 3, 4   *B* 39, 62   *C* 21, 33   *D* 94, 149   *E* 75, 120

9. For which value of n does the expression $n^2 + n + 19$ *not* give a prime number?

   A $n = 6$ *B* $n = 8$ *C* $n = 9$ *D* $n = 11$ *E* $n = 14$

10. You are shipwrecked on an island inhabited by two tribes – Knights (who always tell the truth), and Knaves (who always lie). When captured you are looked after by two friendly jailers called Tweedledum (T_1) and Tweedledee (T_2). They tell you that you could regain your freedom if only you could discover which tribes your two jailers belong to. To help you, Tweedledum says 'We come from different tribes.' But Tweedledee immediately says 'Oh no we don't!'. What can you conclude about your two jailers?

	A	B	C	D	E
T_1 is a	Knight	Knight	Knave	Knave	Can't be sure
T_2 is a	Knight	Knave	Knight	Knave	

PAPER 42

1. To pass a test with 80 questions you have to get 60% correct. Margaret was just three questions short of a pass. How many questions did she answer correctly?

    A 45   *B* 48   *C* 51   *D* 57   *E* 77

2. These two squares have been cut into five pieces. The pieces can be rearranged to make a larger square. What will the perimeter of the larger square be?

    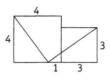

    A 28   *B* 25   *C* 21   *D* 20   *E* 18

3. The 07.28 train from Edinburgh arrives in London at 12.24. It has a two-minute stop at Newcastle and again at York. The track distance from Edinburgh to London is $393\frac{1}{2}$ miles. What is the average speed of the train (in mph) closest to?

    A 30   *B* 60   *C* 80   *D* 104.68   *E* 125

4. Five years ago, Khalia's father was four times as old as her. Now he is three times as old as she is. How many more years will it be before Khalia's father is only twice as old as Khalia?

    A 5   *B* 10   *C* 15   *D* 20   *E* it will never happen

5. The number 82C bus can carry a maximum of 54 people. It starts off empty. At the first stop four people get on. At the second stop one gets off and six get on. At the third two get off and eight get on. And so on – the number getting on increases by two at each stop while the number getting off increases by one. How many get on at the last stop where the bus can pick up passengers while still following this rule?

    A 8   *B* 10   *C* 12   *D* 14   *E* 16

6. Two circular discs with radii 4 cm and 3 cm intersect at right angles. If the overlapping portions are removed, what is the difference between the two remaining areas?

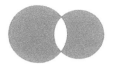

A 7π cm^2 B 2π cm^2 C 7 cm^2 D π cm^2 E hard to say

7. Which of the following numbers has an odd number of factors?

A 33 B 34 C 35 D 36 E 37

8. I want to assemble twenty-seven unit cubes into a strong $3 \times 3 \times 3$ cube. Wherever two small cubes meet face to face I shall put glue on one of these two faces. How many small faces do I have to put glue on?

A 18 B 27 C 36 D 54 E 108

9. The library book I am reading has 720 pages. The day I borrowed it I read exactly half. The next day I read one-third of what was left. On the day after that I read one-quarter of what remained. What fraction of the book remained unread?

A $\frac{1}{2}$ B $\frac{1}{3}$ C $\frac{1}{4}$ D $\frac{1}{5}$ E $\frac{1}{6}$

10. Which of the following digits cannot be one of the missing digits in the multiplication shown here?

A 3 B 4 C 6 D 8 E 9

$$\begin{array}{r} \text{\_ \_} \\ \text{\_ \_} \times \\ \hline \text{\_ \_ \_} \\ 5\ \text{\_} \\ \hline -5\ 5\ - \\ \hline \end{array}$$

ANSWERS TO SECTION B

PAPER 1

A	A	E	E	E
C	E	D	E	D

PAPER 2

C	C	C	D	E
D	C	B	E	E

PAPER 3

A	B	D	E	B
B	B	E	C	C

PAPER 4

D	B	C	A	D
B	E	B	C	E

PAPER 5

B	E	B	D	B
E	C	E	B	B

PAPER 6

D	B	E	D	C
B	E	E	D	E

PAPER 7

D	C	B	D	E
D	D	D	A	E

PAPER 8

D	C	C	C	E
B	B	D	B	D

PAPER 9

A	D	C	B	B
D	A	B	E	E

PAPER 10

B	D	D	E	D
C	E	C	B	D

PAPER 11

E	A	B/E	C	A
D	B	C	C	D

PAPER 12

D	E	B	A	C
B	B	B	B	E

PAPER 13

E	E	B	A	B
D	A	E	B	D

PAPER 14

C	E	B	C	C
D	E	A	C	D

PAPER 15

D	D	D	B	C
B	D	E	C	C

PAPER 16

E	D	E	B	B
E	B	E	D	C

PAPER 17

C	B	E	D	A
C	E	C	B	E

PAPER 18

D	D	E	B	A
E	C	C	C	A

PAPER 19

C	A	E	D	C
D	C	A	E	C

PAPER 20

E	C	D	B	A
B	C	D	D	D

PAPER 21

C	C	D	B	C
D	A	E	C	D

PAPER 22

C	A	B	D	B
A	A	D	B	D

PAPER 23

D	D	A	D	B
C	B	D	C	B

PAPER 24

E	C	E	E	D
E	D	E	B	B

PAPER 25

C	D	A/E	E	D
B	E	D	A	E

PAPER 26

E	A	A	C	A
B	D	C	C	B

PAPER 27

C	B	B	B	C
E	B	C	D	E

PAPER 28

D	A	D	D	D
C	B	B	C	C

PAPER 29

C	B	A	D	E
C	A	E	A	C

PAPER 30

D	A	E	E	A
C	D	E	A	D

PAPER 31

E	E	E	D	D
D	A	E	D	B

PAPER 32

B	C	D	B	D
C	E	E	D	C

PAPER 33

D	E	D	C	E
D	B	C	E	E

PAPER 34

B	B	B	C	D
E	D	B	B	B

PAPER 35

D	E	A	D	D
C	C	B	E	D

PAPER 36

B	B	D	D	D
E	E	D	D	E

PAPER 37

D	B	D	D	A
D	E	C	E	A

PAPER 38

E	D	C	E	E
A	E	C	D	C

PAPER 39

B	C	A	D	B
E	B	B	D	B

PAPER 40

D	C	D	E	D
B	E	C	E	D

PAPER 41

E	A	D	D	B
A	D	D	B	B

PAPER 42

A	D	C	C	E
A	D	D	C	D

EPILOGUE

Onions can make you cry, but they don't half improve the stew!

The problems in this collection are not referenced to any particular 'National Curriculum'. Their chief justification is that they make pupils *think* in simple, but important, ways about key mathematical ideas.

Whatever their purpose, none of the problems are routine. They all require students to select appropriate methods, to sift information, and to combine two or more steps. The problems are nevertheless *succinct*: in seeking to stimulate young minds nothing is gained, and much tends to be lost, by too much irrelevant 'noise'. And where a context is used it is more likely to draw on, and appeal to, students' *imagination* than to pay lip-service to the 'real world'. Nevertheless there are plenty of problems which emphasise the link between mathematics and the real world.

The mathematical ingredients needed to solve many of the problems are relatively simple:

What is the value of $19 \times (9 - 0) - (199 + 0) + 19 + 90 \div (1 \times 9 + 9 \times 0)$?
(Paper 9, Question 1)

How many diagonals does a decagon have? (Paper 1, Question 2)

What is the only prime number in the nineties? (Paper 19, Question 4)

What is the angle between the hands of a clock at quarter to three?
(Paper 23, Question 10)

What is one-third of 299? (Paper 2, Question 1)

What is the smallest possible size of the smallest angle
in a triangle if the largest angle is 85°? (Paper 10, Question 3)

But in none of the problems can the student resort to a conditioned reflex by merely applying some one-step routine. The relevant methods may be within reach, but they have to be chosen carefully and used correctly.

What is the area of a circle with circumference C? (Paper 2, Question 6)

The circumference of a circle or disc is easily measured approximately (by using cotton or string, or, for a very large circle, by pacing round the outside). How can one then calculate the area? It is a very natural question, with a nice answer. But how often is it asked?

One rod of length 10, two of length 9, and so on. What is the total length?
(Paper 4, Question 5)

The answer can certainly be calculated the hard way. But the question has a *structure* which turns out to be the same as that of a much better known problem:

Chords are drawn joining twelve points round a circle.
A thirteenth point is added and all twelve new chords are drawn.
How many extra crossing points can one expect?

Some questions are designed to provoke (possibly lighthearted) discussion: for example Paper 2, Question 4; Paper 4, Question 10; Paper 6, Question 4. Thus

What is the first day of the 21st century? (Paper 2, Question 4)

raises the question of which century the year 2000 belongs to. Other problems raise more serious mathematical points. For example, in mathematics words often have rather different meanings from those in colloquial speech: there are good reasons for this which need to be squarely faced.

What is the total surface area of this open-topped box? (Paper 11, Question 3)

In real life it may seem natural to include both the *inside* and the *outside* 'surface'. However, in mathematics 'surface area' *never* distinguishes the inside and the outside – it only measures the area of an infinitely thin 'layer' or 'membrane'.

Some cats have whiskers. (Paper 15, Question 9)

In colloquial speech the word 'some' is interpreted as 'some, *but not all*'; in mathematics the word 'some' means 'there exists *at least one*'. Thus in mathematics, the statement 'some triangles have three vertices' is true.

Some of the problems may seem a mite ambitious. For example:

In which order should one calculate 10% discount, 17.5% VAT and 12% service charge in order to land up with the least to pay? (Paper 3, Question 4)

and

Roughly how many million seconds have you been alive?
(No calculators!) (Paper 4, Question 9)

But mathematics begins where the sledgehammer leaves off. Thus one should always assume that such problems conceal some *key idea*, which is both more reliable and more instructive than slavishly 'testing all possibilities'.

We have provided answers, but not 'solutions', in the hope that those who use the problems will approach them with an open mind. A good problem is like an onion – with layer upon layer of meaning just waiting to be uncovered. To print one particular solution deprives both teachers and pupils of the experience of peeling off these layers for themselves. At first sight

> *Six toffees in each egg chosen from three sorts, with at least one of each sort in each egg: how many different selections?* (Paper 1, Question 10)

may appear to invite pupils to list all possibilities. Such listing has its value as long as it is *systematic*. Unsystematic approaches are worthless, in that pupils inevitably make mistakes and never notice. A systematic approach may still make mistakes, but can be easily checked and corrected, or improved. But making a systematic list is only the outer skin of the onion. Listing all possibilities soon becomes tedious; it also misses the main point of mathematics, which is not just to grind out answers, but to gain *insight* into efficient, reliable ways of *calculating*!

Thus one would like able pupils to demand something better – such as the fact that three of the six toffees in each egg are predetermined ('*at least one of each sort*'). If one puts these three toffees in each egg first, one is left with the simpler problem of *choosing just three toffees of three sorts in any way one wishes*. At this point one may still need to resort to systematic listing, but one has used an *idea* to simplify the selections being listed (from six toffees to three toffees) so one is less likely to go astray. There is no need to stop there. With older, or more able, students one can peel off further layers and explore general methods for choosing n toffees of r different sorts (where repetition is allowed and order does not matter).

Similarly, at first sight

> *What is the largest amount I cannot make with 5p and 11p stamps?*
> (Paper 4, Question 6)

may appear to involve simple testing of each option. Again such testing has its value as long as it is systematic. A systematic approach can be easily checked and, if necessary, corrected; an unsystematic approach cannot.

Testing each number of pence in turn to see whether it can be obtained by combining 5s and 11s may provide good practice in arithmetic. But it is unlikely to provide 'insight into efficient, reliable ways of calculating'. In this instance there are more interesting things lurking just below the surface. One of the reasons mathematics is important is that one often finds totally unexpected structures behind what looks like an innocuous problem. The serious, but elementary, mathematics behind this problem is explored at length in my book *Discovering Mathematics* (Oxford University Press, 1987).

The experience of using these problems should provide teachers with much food for thought. The problems *assume* that pupils have already achieved *fluency* in those basic techniques which are fundamental to all elementary mathematics. This crucial basic fluency can only be achieved the hard way – through clear exposition, much practice, and strict insistence on complete accuracy. There are no short cuts. Fortunately youngsters enjoy mastering, and using, standard arithmetical, algebraic and geometrical techniques. Those who have argued that, in the age of calculators and software packages, we no longer need to insist on complete fluency in mastering tables, standard arithmetical algorithms, fractions, ratio, proportion, algebra, elementary Euclidean and coordinate geometry, or whatever have misconstrued the way human beings learn mathematics, and have inadvertently sold a whole generation short.

The step from exercising routine, one-step skills in familiar settings to handling genuine multi-step *problems* is never easy. But it is no more difficult than mastering other complex skills, and can be achieved in the same way – by a combination of motivation and *repeated* practice. Thus our pupils need lots of *short*, multi-step problems: that is, they need as much experience of tackling and solving short, challenging, specific (i.e. closed!) problems as we can possibly provide. Of course, one would also like youngsters to have the experience of exploring longer, more open, problems; but this kind of activity is a relative luxury and should never be allowed to displace the more basic task of tackling lots of short, multi-step problems.

Regrettably, many fundamental topics which used to provide pupils with the experience of integrating one-step routines to solve simple multi-step problems (e.g. subtraction; short and long division; simplifying fractions, mixed surds, expressions involving powers, and algebraic expressions; factorising quadratics; angle-chasing; congruence and similarity; applications of Pythagoras' Theorem in three dimensions) have recently been downplayed, or even declared to be obsolete, without apparently appreciating the pedagogical consequences.

Problems such as those in this collection, or in my book *Mathematical Puzzling* (Oxford University Press, 1987), can help to fill the resulting vacuum. But occasional puzzles are no substitute for a good staple diet. Thus one must hope that the coming years will see a radical review of what should lie at the heart of the standard curriculum.

For EU product safety concerns, contact us at Calle de José Abascal, 56–1°, 28003 Madrid, Spain or eugpsr@cambridge.org.